THE KENT STATE
MUSEUM

THE KENT STATE
MUSEUM

Martha Pullen's Favorite Places Series

The Martha Pullen Company

Publisher: Martha Pullen

Editorial Direction by Jean Druesedow

Written by Jean Druesedow

Editorial Contribution by Amelia Johanson

Embroidery Art by Angela Pullen Atherton

Photography by Kate Rieppel

✦ ✦ ✦ ✦ ✦ ✦ ✦ ✦

The Martha Pullen Company
149 Old Big Cove Road
Brownsboro, Alabama 35741
www.marthapullen.com

Hoffman Media, LLC.

President: Phyllis Hoffman

Production Direction by Greg Baugh

Graphic Design by Karissa Brown

Color Correction by Delisa McDaniel

✦ ✦ ✦ ✦ ✦ ✦ ✦ ✦

Hoffman Media, LLC.
1900 International Park Drive, Suite 50
Birmingham, Alabama 35243

Printed in the United States of America

ISBN: 978-0-9794090-9-7

CONTENTS

Bows and Lace Afternoon Dress............................ 15

Chiffon and Silk Flowers Afternoon Ensemble 16

Ayrshire Appliqué Christening Gown 20

Swirls of Eyelet Capelet-Collar Coat 22

Silver Sequined Ball Gown.................................... 24

Ruffled Tucks, Lace and Flowers Dress.................. 26

Eyelet Stars Toddler Dress 28

Medallion and Daisies Wedding Gown 30

Passementerie Open Robe Christening Gown 32

Blue Green Ribbon Dress 34

Dropped Waist Eyelet Dress with
Shoulder Flounce 38

Simple Baby Doll Dress 40

Golden Silk Gown.. 42

Bleeding Heart Christening Gown......................... 44

Irish Crochet Toddler Dress................................... 46

Long Waisted Teen Dress 48

Tiers of Pink Ruffles Dress.................................... 50

Floral Vine Christening Gown............................... 52

Embroidered Bird Baby Dress 54

Ornamented Wool Tea Gown................................ 56

Embroidered Black Velvet Fauntleroy Suit............ 58

Embroidered Net Dress 60

White Cotton and Lace Summer
Matinée Dress 62

Ivory Net Tea Dress... 64

Wild Rose White Piqué Coat 66

Ribbon-Striped Dimity and Lace Dress 68

Butterfly Sleeves Dress... 70

Neo-Classic Greek Key Ayrshire
Christening Gown 72

Ruffled Chantilly Lace Dress................................. 74

Bleeding Heart Embroidery Blouse....................... 76

Circle of Tulle Dress 78

Ecru Silk Dress with Lace Swirls and
Fabric Roses... 80

Crepe Dress with Blue Smocking 84

Rickrack Birthday Party Dress 86

Champagne Bridesmaid's Dress 88

Vertical Tucks and Broderie Anglaise Dress.......... 90

Filet Lace Heirloom Peignoir 92

Sleeveless Angled Yoke Pinafore 94

Vertical Stripes of Puffing Dress........................... 96

White Dotted Net and Lace Summer Lingerie
Dress and Shawl 98

Velvet-Trimmed Dress Coat................................. 100

Basic Yoke Dress with Gold Buttons.................... 102

Delicate Blue Flowers Afternoon Dress............... 104

Latticework Baby Bubble 106

Raspberry Silk Evening Dress.............................. 108

Shark's Tooth Christening Gown 110

Point d'esprit and Lace Triangles Dress 112

Blue and White Stripes and
Chambray Ensemble 116

Cream Piqué Coat with Leaf Motif Insertion 118

Green Silk Gay Nineties Dress 120

Smocked Toddler's Dress with Elongated
Eyelet Tabs.. 122

Little Boy's Gold Sailor Suit 124

Blue and White Honeycomb Dress...................... 126

Day Dress of Printed Black and White Silk........ 128

Little Girl's Maroon Silk Dress 130

Child's Swirls of Bobbin Lace Petticoat 132

Little Girl's Polka Dot and Eyelet Dress 134

Filet Lace Shawl 136

Tabbed Shoulder Capelet 138

Baby's Butterfly Bibs 140

Turn of the Century Diapers 141

Dedicated to
Dr. Elizabeth Rhodes

Sometimes God sends a friend into my life who seems more like a sister. Elizabeth Rhodes is one of these "God Gifts" to me. With instant camaraderie and a feeling like kinship, we began planning many sewing endeavors between Martha Pullen Company and Kent State University. I have loved the Kent State Museum for many years and this book is a dream come true for me personally as well as for Martha Pullen Company. Since it was Elizabeth who first invited me to the museum, it is with great pleasure that I dedicate this book to her, Dr. Elizabeth Rhodes, Director of the Shannon Rodgers and Jerry Silverman School of Fashion Design and Merchandising at Kent State University in Kent, Ohio.

Martha Pullen

The Kent State
UNIVERSITY MUSEUM

The Kent State University Museum was founded in 1982 when Jerry Silverman and Shannon Rodgers donated their extensive collection of period costumes, designer fashions, furniture, paintings and other objets d'art to the Kent State University Foundation. Their vision was to establish a museum of costume and decorative art and create a school of fashion design and merchandising. The museum is housed in Rockwell Hall, built in 1927 in the Beaux Arts style as the first university library. The building was renovated to conform to the highest museum standards without sacrificing the many outstanding architectural features. The museum opened to the public in October 1985 with nine galleries,

a 120-seat auditorium, a video theatre, storage and exhibition preparation areas and staff offices. The museum works closely with academic units across the University, especially the adjacent Shannon Rodgers and Jerry Silverman School of Fashion Design and Merchandising, allowing students ready access to the galleries and collections. The museum provides the campus and the wider community with a program of changing exhibitions and special events.

In the 1960s, Shannon Rodgers began collecting what is now considered one of the largest and finest period costume collections in the United States. Together with the furnishings of Silverman and Rodgers' homes, it forms one of the world's most comprehensive teaching collections of fashionable design from the 18th century to the present. The original Silverman/Rodgers gift included some 5,000 objects

and an extensive reference library. Today, the museum cares for over 20,000 objects, and the collection continues to grow. The fragile nature of the costume artifacts mandates a program of changing thematic exhibitions. Objects not on exhibition may be studied by appointment with a member of the museum staff.

JERRY SILVERMAN (1911-1984), a native of New York City, left the legal profession to work in the fashion industry at Martini Designs where he became part owner, vice president and sales manager. After service in World War II, he hired another ex-serviceman, SHANNON RODGERS (1910-1996), as the firm's designer. In 1959, Silverman and Rodgers formed their own company, Jerry Silverman, Inc., manufacturing women's better dresses under the label "Shannon Rodgers for Jerry Silverman." Jerry Silverman was a shrewd businessman who never lost sight of his customer. Shannon Rodgers was able to distill the fashionable styles of the haute couture into ready-to-wear dresses that met the needs of the fashionable American woman's lifestyle. Their business partnership became one of the most successful in the fashion industry, a position it maintained for more than 20 years.

Shannon Rodgers was born in Newcomerstown, Ohio. Encouraged to pursue a career in the arts, he began by working in the New York theatre as an assistant to the costume designer, Woodman Thompson. He made extra money by sketching in the fashion industry. Cecil B. DeMille hired him to work in Hollywood on the 1932 production of Cleopatra. During the years before World War II, he worked for almost all the major Hollywood studios as a studio artist. In New York, after the war, while looking for a job in advertising, he found himself on Seventh Avenue where a friend suggested he apply for a fashion design position available at Martini Designs. Reluctant at first, he finally did apply and was hired by Jerry Silverman.

• • • • • • • •

For The Kent State University Museum hours and information, call 330-672-3450 or visit www.kent.edu/museum.

10 | KENT STATE MUSEUM

Kent State
CONTRIBUTORS

ELIZABETH A. RHODES, PH.D.

Director, The Fashion School, Kent State University

Elizabeth Ann Jones was born in Louisville, Kentucky on April 4, 1947. She was the oldest child of three and the only girl. Her mother, grandmothers and aunts all sewed, so it was only natural that at a very young age she took up a needle.

When she was a girl, her family moved to rural western North Carolina where the textile industry operated major factories. She recalls Stonecutter Mills where they emptied scraps down a shoot into a large wooden box twice a day. If she were there, she could get wonderful fabric for 25 cents a yard. She was often there. Another place she frequented was Doncaster's outlet, which was in the back of a greasy corner service station but had silk linen, long-staple cottons and fine fabrics. She learned textiles from experience at the outlets of major factories.

As a young person, Elizabeth was a 4-H member. The club played an integral role in establishing a base for her professional and sewing interests. Leaders in 4-H taught sewing techniques and encouraged her to enter dress reviews and other competitions.

In high school, Elizabeth had three years of Home Economics. The unit on sewing was always her favorite, as she enjoyed the challenge of converting 2-D fabric to a 3-D garment. She mastered the seam ripper out of necessity, but soon realized how much more rewarding it was to do things right the first time.

In 1965, Elizabeth enrolled at Berea College to major in Home Economics and was encouraged by her counselors not to pursue a career that involved sewing. She quietly continued to make nearly all her apparel, and followed what was suggested to be a more lucrative plan of study. Today, she has come to admire women like Sue Hausmann of Husqvarna Viking and Martha Pullen who "thumbed their noses" at the world and proved that sewing is an honorable career.

Many years later, after completing a Ph.D. in Consumer Behavior, Elizabeth became the director of The Shannon Rodgers and Jerry Silverman School of Fashion Design and Merchandising. She has been married more than 40 years, has two grown children and three grandchildren. She sews now for creative expression and to do something special for her family and friends.

During the 1970s, through her university ties, Elizabeth met Charles Kleibacker an American designer who was dubbed "Master of the Bias." Elizabeth invited Mr. Kleibacker to Kent each summer to conduct workshops, and by "handing him the pins," she learned about draping, bias construction and couture techniques. In fact, once she was exposed to couture ateliers, she realized how many home economics techniques of the 1950-60s were couture-based.

The 1980s provided Elizabeth with the opportunity to take groups of students and adults to Europe for study tours where they were privileged to go into couture houses and observe techniques. The opportunity was invaluable as many of those fine houses are closed today signaling the end of an era. During these visits, she was able to take people to study beading and embroidery at the House of Lesage in Paris. Then, in 1994 and 1995, she arranged for Mr. Lesage and his workers to teach in the United States. Kent State University was the first and only site to host the designer's classes in this country.

As director of The Shannon Rodgers and Jerry Silverman School of Fashion Design and Merchandising, Elizabeth oversees more than a thousand students and promotes this jewel in Ohio to the industry. She has worked with the faculty to expand the offerings of the school so that students have studio space in New York City for a semester of their work as well as the opportunity to study a semester in Europe using the KSU Florence campus as their home base. She has taken study tours to China and has established an exchange program with Hong Kong Polytechnic University.

Elizabeth continues to sew regularly and learned to embroider by machine about a decade ago. After being introduced to the newest technology, she treated herself to a top model machine, and, as they say, the rest is history.

JEAN LAWRENCE DRUESEDOW

Author
Director, Kent State
University Museum

I have been told that I started to sew on the machine at age 3—without the needle—that by the time I was 5, my mother put the needle in the machine, and I know that I have been happily sewing ever since. I have taken great delight in teaching five little granddaughters to sew, and of course, we started when each was 5 with the needle firmly in place. My hope is that they might find the pleasure, the challenge and the sense of accomplishment that I have found sewing.

Learning to sew has ordered the course of my life, first as a theatre student at Indiana University, then as a theatrical costume designer teaching at Miami University in Oxford, Ohio, and at Eastern Kentucky University in Richmond, Kentucky, and finally as a fashion historian and museum director. Life takes us in unexpected directions, and so from the theatre, I found myself, in 1978, a curator at the Costume Institute of the Metropolitan Museum of Art. Since 1993, I have been

the director at the Kent State University Museum, a museum of fashion and decorative arts known throughout the world for the depth and quality of its collection of dress. What an extraordinary opportunity it is to learn about fashion history from the garments themselves, and how lucky students are to be able to see and work with our collection. When you know with your hands as well as your head what fabrics do as you take them from two-dimensional cloth to three-dimensional garments, the understanding of the art of dress is much more complete and meaningful. You know what it takes to make those tiny tucks, to work with silks or wools, to drape and fit a dress just so, and your appreciation of the skilled seamstresses of the past is confirmed.

I hope that as you use this book and explore the wonderful possibilities for decorative sewing within its pages, you will enjoy these amazing pieces as I do, and find in them a means of understanding life and times quite different from our own.

KATE RIEPPEL

Photographer

I first became interested in fashion and costume during my undergraduate career at Smith College where I received a B.A. in Anthropology. While at Smith, I photographed and catalogued many items in the Smith College Historical Costume Collection and served as curator for several small exhibits. In the autumn of 2004, I was privileged to work as a research assistant at the Kent State University Museum on the exhibit Allegory and Symbol, Chinese Robes in the Kent State University Museum Collection. I enjoy studying the relationship between cultural movements and fashion. Photography has been one of my interests since childhood, and it makes perfect sense to combine my love of fashion with visual expression.

Bows & Lace
AFTERNOON DRESS

"Yet, if the production of lace were the result of close and bitter work, that is so much the more reason that it should be well paid for, apart from its immense intrinsic value as a real artistic affair; and this has been so plainly recognized that it has always brought great price, the old Honiton being paid for by laying it out flatly and spreading silver shillings upon it, the maker carrying off as many shillings as were required to cover the whole piece, which, although the promise might at first seem small, made really a good round sum in pounds sterling."

—*Harper's Bazaar*, "Cobwebs of Fashion," (September 1887)

That this gown shares both a sense of drama and romance cannot be lost on a student of early fashion and theater. Famous actresses of the late 19th century, such as Gabriélle Rejane and Sarah Bernhardt, favored all-lace costumes not unlike this glorious example. Their influence would have been felt throughout fashion, just as current celebrities lend relevance to modern-day style. This cotton organdy piece is an elaborately bustled summer afternoon dress from the late 1870s. It has a cream taffeta underdress and combines whitework bands, lace insertion, rows of puffed organdy and satin ribbons. The overdress has long sleeves and opens at the center front with 12 fabric-covered buttons hidden by a lace jabot. The different elements are worked vertically on the bodice and horizontally on the skirt. There are large cream satin bows on the sleeve cuffs, the back of the neck and around the bustle. The underdress has a boned bodice with a standing, pleated ruffle at the neckline and a bustled skirt. It opens in the front with 19 mother-of-pearl buttons and has tiny cap sleeves trimmed with lace at the armholes. The hem is decorated with a layer of lace-trimmed cotton organdy that is visible under the hem of the overdress. The underdress hem is stiffened with a facing of twill-weave cotton and two layers of pleated silk.

{ *Silverman/Rodgers Collection, 1983.1.123ab* }

Chiffon and Silk Flowers
AFTERNOON ENSEMBLE

"White Chantilly lace will be very pretty for the neck and sleeves of evening and bridal gowns. It has been many years since Chantilly lace has been in fashion, and now it is being shown chiefly in white."

—*The Ladies' Home Journal*, "The New Spring Trimmings," (April 1907)

Out-of-door parties and picnics were considered fashionable amusements at the turn of the last century and "fancy styles of dress were worn by both ladies and gentlemen" according to the media of the time. This pretty pink ensemble would have served for such afternoon wear from about 1905. Both the dress and jacket are made from ecru chiffon overlaid with a large mesh, appliquéd with silk cutout in bold scrolling stems, leaves and flowers; embroidered details lend a three-dimensional touch. Additionally the dress bodice has an inset of heavily starched Irish crochet appliquéd on pintucked net, and panels of machine-made Chantilly lace. Pleated bands of silk are placed around the waist and over the shoulders with bows at both front and back. The petticoat is silk with a ruffle at the bottom.

"In this as our American afternoon teas have been managed, the American young lady was right, for it is not convenable, according to European ideas to wear a loose flowing robe of the tea-gown pattern out of one's bedroom or boudoir. It has been done by ignorant people at a watering-place, but it never looks well. It is really an undress, although lace and satin may be used in its composition. A lain, high, and tight fitting garment is much the more elegant dress for the afternoon teas as we give them."

—*Harper's Bazaar,* "Afternoon Tea," (January 1884)

The dress closes at the back with hooks and eyes and with a bow at the center back that has small hanging tassels. The dress has a slight train. The jacket has short kimono-style sleeves and a V-neck opening to the waist where it closes with hooks and eyes. There are 21-inch long silk tassels attached on either side of the front opening. The back of the jacket reaches to the knees.
{ *Gift of Cora Ginsburg, 1989.22.1ab* }

Ayrshire Appliqué
CHRISTENING GOWN

"While inspecting the wardrobe of a newly arrived infant the other day, one of those fortunate children born to daintiness and fine linen, I noticed that the dresses of English nainsook followed the fashion for fine needlework so prevalent, and that the nicer gowns were trimmed with drawn work, hem-stitching, and featherstitching, or fine embroidery and lace."

—*The Cosmopolitan*, "Fashions for the Little Ones," (February 1887)

Judging by the placement of the Ayrshire embroidered oval—the centerpiece around which the yoke of this christening gown is framed—it held a special meaning for the child or the seamstress. It is the only Ayrshire work on the gown, and was likely cut from another source, roughly encircled

with lace edging and appliquéd onto the yoke. The bodice on this 19th century piece is further embroidered with featherstitching and French knots, echoing the shape of the Ayrshire appliqué. There is an oval of lace insertion on the front yoke that surrounds a symmetrical array of embroidered flowers and leaves. This christening gown is 38-inches long and 64-inches around the hem. The sleeves are slightly puffed and are decorated with an upward point of lace insertion and embroidery. The back of the bodice is detailed with three groups of three $^1/_8$-inch pleats alternating with $^5/_8$-inch of fabric embroidered down the center with featherstitching on each side of the center back. On the skirt, 17-inches from the bodice, is a panel of alternating diagonal strips of lace insertion and embroidery. It is bordered at both top and bottom by a strip of floral and geometric patterned embroidery. It is not whipped into an entredeux edge as we would do today. The hem flounce is gathered and tucked in groups of seven pleats every 4-inches. It is eyelet embroidery with tiny flowers and dots and is finished with a scalloped edge.

{ Gift of Martha McCaskey Selhorst Collection, 2003.35.20 }

Swirls of Eyelet
CAPELET-COLLAR COAT

"They are so fresh, unhackneyed and so full of real artistic beauty that one can use any and every one of them with the full assurance that the style is one that will hold a long time."

—*Pictorial Review*, "Pretty Fashions in Children's Coats," (June 1900)

This little coat embodies elegance for obvious reasons. The swirl of eyelet worked around large open flowers is a picture of triumphant needlework. The silhouette is of equal appeal with its wide cape collar that dramatically reaches to the cuffs. The coat is composed of two widths of eyelet 5-inches and 1³/₄-inches wide. The wide eyelet is used for the bottom and center fronts and is cleverly pieced at the corners. The narrow eyelet is alternated with 2¹/₈-inch strips of batiste to form vertical stripes that make up the body of the cape collar, the skirt of the coat and the cuffs. The neckline is finished with a mandarin collar of eyelet lined with cotton. The bodice under the wide cape collar is made of an eyelet fabric embroidered with a small floral pattern and has two ⁵/₈-inch tucks on each side of the center front, center back and French seams. The seams at the waist, armscye, cuffs, neckband and the inside edge of the wide eyelet are all piped. The coat buttons with four ³/₄-inch buttons. It is American from about 1900. A "w" is embroidered inside the neckband, which could be the child's initial or the signature mark of the maker. { *Gift of Martha McCaskey Selhorst Collection, 2003.35.5* }

Silver Sequined
BALL GOWN

"In the 'glittering horseshoe' of boxes at the opera this season white toilettes prevail with gowns of white and gold, or white and silver, white with Russian sable, or else that latest expression of the Paris modiste's art, white tulle strewn with diamond dust. The pearl white, called 'oyster shell white,' is chosen for young women, especially for blondes, while softer creamy tints are more becoming to brunettes and to those who are older."

—Harper's Bazaar, "New York Fashions," (January 1890)

Opera in the late 19th century was a gala affair attended by smartly dressed couples. Gowns mirrored the stunning architecture typical of theatrical surroundings. According to New York fashion magazines of the times, bodices of opera gowns would have been draped with great "elaborateness, spangled with silver or gold details," not unlike this English ball gown from about 1900. Worn across the sea during the same era, this piece is labeled Madame Parmentier, Court Dressmaker, 1 Lower Belgrave Street, Belgravia, S.W. It is white tulle and Duchesse lace appliqué on a machine net ground trimmed with cloth of silver, silver sequins, opalescent sequins and pearls. The low, formal, lace-trimmed neckline reveals the shoulders. The short, puffed sleeves, which cover the upper arms, are made of nine tulle ruffles spangled with tiny silver sequins and stitched to a tulle under sleeve. After the first four ruffles, there are two bands of silver lamé bordering a band of the tulle undersleeve, then five more ruffles. The bodice has three layers of fabric. The first is a creamy silk taffeta, the next is tulle spangled with silver sequins, and the top layer is Duchesse lace appliqué. There is a diagonal line of three-dimensional opalescent and silver sequined flowers, trailing tiny pearl vines, appliquéd around the back neckline, over the right shoulder, ending at the left side of the waist. A waistband of silver lamé comes to a point in front. The bodice opens at the back with hooks and eyes. There are five flowers along the back opening made from silver thread. The skirt has the same three layers of fabric as the bodice. The under layer of heavy creamy silk has a dust ruffle that is decorated with three bands of silver lamé at the hem.

{ *Silverman/Rodgers Collection, 1983.1.228ab* }

Ruffled Tucks,
LACE AND FLOWERS DRESS

"Just a word as to the length of skirts. For the younger girls I prefer the skirt to clear the floor; while for older girls or matrons a pretty length is to have the skirt just touch all around. With either of these lengths one's dainty petticoat would answer as a drop skirt or there may be used a foundation skirt of white lawn finished with a ruffled or plaited flounce. When the outside skirt is of greater length a drop skirt is absolutely necessary."

—*The Ladies' Home Journal,* "Mrs Holden's Talks with the Girl
who Makes Her Own Clothes," (August 1904)

Mrs. Holden, in her "Talks With the Girl Who Makes Her Own Clothes," (*Ladies' Home Journal*, August 1904) advises her readers that "pretty flower-sprigged, figured, striped and dotted lawns, dimities, or-gandies and Swiss muslins are to be found at prices so low that the possession of a necessary or an extra gown is quite a simple matter." It may be simple, in theory, perhaps, but certainly not in execution, judging by this Edwardian dress from the same time period. It is neither simple in construction nor decoration. It is made from sheer cotton printed with delicate pink hydrangeas with green leaves, and trimmed with white chemical lace and white linen eyelet. The exquisitely feminine bodice of this one-piece dress has a high-standing lace collar trimmed in white linen eyelet and a narrow pink silk ribbon. The upper part of the yoke is embroidered tulle and lace, edged in the linen eyelet. The bodice is softly drawn with five rows of gathers, and it is trimmed with lace, eyelet and lace "flowers" centered with crocheted balls. The sleeves are elbow-length and slightly puffed with eight rows of gathers along the inner arm that draw up the length of the sleeve to the elbow; four rows of horizontal gathers alternate with three 1-inch tucks to draw in the width of the sleeve to fit the arm below the elbow. Lace decorates the dress above and below the waist. Eleven inches below the waist is the first of two bands of lace separated by a 2-inch band of the printed fabric; the first lace band is $2^1/_4$-inches wide, and the second $3^1/_4$-inches wide. About 15-inches above the hemline is a set of ruffled $^1/_4$-inch tucks and one 1-inch tuck like the ones on the sleeves, and 5-inches below that are five horizontal tucks, each $^1/_2$-inch wide. The last tuck is 3-inches above the hem. The dress opens in the back from the collar to the waist and is closed with hooks and eyes. It was altered for contemporary wear by adding a strip of another bobbin lace down the center back opening to expand the bodice. Little crocheted tassels were also added at the center back waist.

{ *Gift of Helen O. Borowitz, 2004.25.1* }

Eyelet Stars TODDLER DRESS

"Great Value in a Child's Embroidery Dress. The front is made of wide embroidery a scalloped edge outlining front of the neck. The skirt is made of pretty embroidery flouncing through which messaline ribbon is drawn and tied in a bow. Sleeves finish with embroidery beading, silk ribbon and val. Edging. Color: white only. Sizes: 2-6 years. Prepaid $1.35."

—Philipsborn Spring and Summer Catalogue, 1914

The eyelet pattern fashioned on this toddler dress from about 1915 gives the impression of a night sky filled with stars—a star light, star bright motif echoing a favorite childhood verse. The effect could have been intentional or simply a bonus, perhaps pointed out by the child herself who might have favored her "star" dress. The piece is hand-worked cotton eyelet. The front and the back have three panels of 2-inch eyelet lace that alternate with $1^{1}/_{4}$-inch panels of white cotton with three vertical tucks each. The waist of the dress has eyelet lace loops that serve as belt loops to hold a ribbon. The skirt of the dress is gathered at the waist. One-half inch under the waist, there are three $^{1}/_{8}$-inch tucks spaced $^{5}/_{16}$-inch apart. The skirt is made of a larger scale eyelet with a $4^{1}/_{2}$-inch scalloped border. The long sleeves are puffed and decorated with eyelet and lace at the wrists. The collar is made of eyelet and is edged with a $^{1}/_{2}$-inch piece of gathered lace. The bodice of the dress opens at the back with a placket that has loops hidden underneath to hide the buttons, which was a typical treatment of the time.

{ Gift of Martha McCaskey Selhorst Collection, 2003.35.26 }

Medallion and Daisies
WEDDING GOWN

"The bride and her bridesmaids, whether attired in expensive satin or simple muslin, may be as dainty and picturesque as the heart of anyone can desire."

—*The Ladies' Home Journal*, "The Easter Bride and Her Bridesmaids," (March 1901)

This 1903 wedding gown was made in New York City and is labeled L.P. Hollander & Co., Costumers, 200 Fifth Avenue. It is made from a large mesh silk net and is ornamented with pintucks and embroidered lace insertion. The bodice has a high-standing collar and sleeves puffed at the elbow and tight to the wrist, closing with two buttons. There is a large medallion on the front center bodice under the collar that continues into a vertical strip of the lace insert. Both the bodice and skirt are made of alternating vertical strips of the lace insertion and vertically pintucked net. The embroidered lace inserts have vine, daisy-like flower and lattice motifs that are somewhat oriental in design. A *Godey's Ladies' Book* article published a decade earlier and addressing the fashion in Paris makes particular note of the "exhibitions of beautiful antique embroideries of the East." It describes the intricacies of Chinese embroideries and an exquisite Japanese lady's robe. *Harper's Bazaar*, a decade after this wedding gown was worn, describes the "kimono" lines of a reception gown. Clearly, fashion's fondness for Asian design inspiration and fabrication is timeless, as it is equally relevant today. In addition to being decorated with rows of the Asian lattice and daisy-embroidered motifs, the skirt of this gown has two under-layers, one of organza with three rows of 1-inch ruffles at the hem and one of taffeta with a gathered ruffle at the hem. These under-layers lend volume to the skirt hem. The outer skirt has four barely-full flounces at the hem, each trimmed with three rows of satin ribbon.

{ *Transferred from the Allen Memorial Art Museum, Oberlin College, Oberlin, Ohio. Gift of Betty L. More through Edith Metcalf, 1953, 1995.17.356ab* }

Passementerie Open Robe
CHRISTENING GOWN

"Do all sewing, not only for yourself, but for your children (which distinction is too often made) strongly, nicely, and neatly. Don't be afraid of setting too many stitches in the seams of a garment, nor spending too much time in setting them in properly. Let your work be such that you will never be ashamed to have it examined, in fact something that you will be pleased and proud to have closely scrutinized."

—*The New England Farmer*, "Children's Clothes," (August 1868)

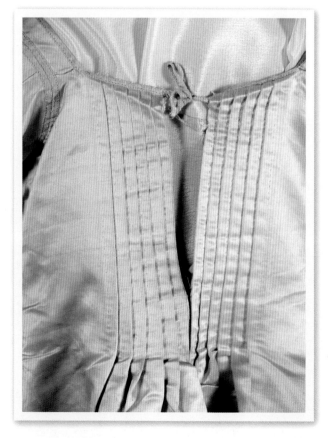

A newly arrived infant of means, born in the fourth quarter of the 18th century would have been lavished in silk on his or her christening day. This being an open-robe design, it would have been worn over a gown, perhaps less elaborately trimmed.

The lovely creamy silk satin robe is decorated with a passementerie of looped fringe, scallops and fly fringe, as well as grosgrain ribbon bows, which sweetly secure the robe down center front. The passementerie is about $1^1/_2$-inches wide and winds in an elegant serpentine down the bodice of the dress and along the hem of the gown. It also adorns the petite, turned-back cuffs on the sleeves. The bodice is pleated on the front and the back from the shoulders down to the waist. The pleats are set every $1/_4$-inch. There are 10 on the back that create lovely lines down the back of the skirt as if to mimic the *robe á la anglaise* of the mother. The square neckline and hip fullness are also reflective of the mother's dress. The neckline, armscye and shoulder straps are bound with a narrow grosgrain ribbon.

{ *Silverman/Rodgers Collection, 1983.1.1* }

Blue Green
RIBBON DRESS

"Sashes will be very much worn this year with all summer clothes of the sheerer variety, such as organdies, lawns and Swisses; in fact, they are the prettiest and daintiest way of finishing the waist."

—*The Ladies' Home Journal*, "Mrs. Ralston's Chat," (June 1905)

The idea of "sheer elegance" was most assuredly inspired by a dress like this one. The waistband treatment alone suggests a design sense beyond the average seamstress's capabilities; a taffeta ribbon is both ingeniously and elegantly secured by an embroidered piece of cotton in a zigzag pattern that echoes the V line executed on the bodice of the gown. The embroidered lace yoke establishes the V line; it runs over each shoulder and comes to a point at center front. Additional embroidery is slightly angled on the remainder of the bodice, as is the placement of three-dimensional, embroidered posies. The zigzag of embroidery on the sash extends into the skirt yoke, which like the bodice yoke, finishes in a point at center front. The V effect is sharply contrasted in the remainder of the skirt, which is worked in horizontal bands of the various fabrics and a center column of embroidery and posies. The zigzag effect is revisited at the very edge of the hemline. Taken in its entirety, this piece, from

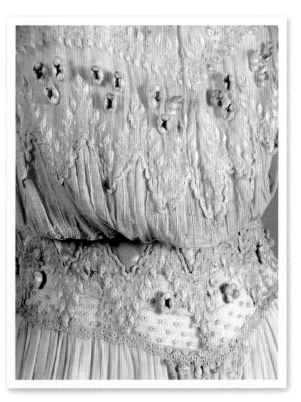

about 1907, is an extremely pretty summer afternoon dress. The materials consist of sheer white embroidered cotton, sheer tucked cotton, plain cotton, embroidered lace and three-dimensional flowers appliquéd on the embroidered panels. The pale ribbon worked into the waistband is gathered into a frou-frou at center back; it is draped into the sleeves just above the lace cuffs. The elbow-length sleeves are also decorated with alternating bands of embroidered cotton, lace insertion and gathered edging, tucked cotton and plain cotton. The skirt ends in a slight train. The dress opens down the back with hooks and eyes.

{ Gift of the Fine Arts Association, Willoughby, Ohio, 1994.65.8 }

Dropped Waist Eyelet
DRESS WITH SHOULDER FLOUNCE

". . . we honestly think that many an hour spent in first making and then ironing and doing up the perfectly useless flounces and puffs of an elaborate little dress might be better spent in giving to the child that sympathy which a mother alone possess—only a mother can give."

—Ohio Farmer, "Children's Clothes," (May 1875)

The stylish and becoming flounces that run from dropped waistband to waistband over the shoulders give the clever illusion of a separate pinafore. In reality, it is a basic dropped waist design with front fullness and an elongated silhouette typical of the early 1900s. The sweet and frilly dress was presumably reserved for a child of 7 or 8 to wear to church and other special occasions. The eyelets—insertion and wide edging—serve to finish all of the garment edges whether it be the square neckline created by the positioning of insertions or the sleeve and skirt edges primed with the elegant scalloped design of the eyelet border. The dress is cotton as are the eyelets. The neckline and the seams of the vertical flounces on both the front and back are appliquéd with the 1-inch embroidered insertion that coordinates with the border pattern of the main fabric. Delicately peeping out from behind the eyelet at the hem is an edging of bobbin lace, which may have been original to the dress or added to extend the length.

{ Collection of Ruth and Ralph Fuller, donated by his sister, Elsie Joy, P.O.A., 1992.21.17 }

Simple
BABY DOLL DRESS

"First clothes for babies have become so short that they can no longer be properly called "long clothes" as the longest dress is not more than twenty-six or twenty-eight inches in length, barely reaching to the child's toes."

—*The Ladies' Home Journal,* "Mrs. Ralston's Chat About Children's Clothes," (July 1906)

In describing a baby wardrobe from the turn of the 20th century, *The Cosmpolitan* magazine writes of "sleeves made so as to cover the arms, were gathered a little full at top and bottom and finished in the same way as the neck." On this simple baby doll dress of the period, the seamstress may have attempted to follow that dictate; the sleeves are indeed long and gathered at the shoulder and wrist, but she fell short of embellishing them adequately. The cuffs are finished with a $^{1}/_{4}$-inch wide bias band that is topped with an equal width of lace insertion. The insertion is only stitched to the upper edge of the cuff band; the lower edge of the lace is not finished with an edging, as would be a more traditional treatment. On the contrary, the neckline, yoke flounce and skirt are finished with a narrow edging. An assumption could be made that the seamstress did not have enough edging to finish the cuffs and so rather than leave them unadorned, settled on using the insertion. This little dress is primarily machine sewn and is made of white cotton batiste and $^{1}/_{2}$-inch strips of lace insertion. The body of the dress is made of two pieces of fabric that are gathered to the yoke. The round yoke is made from vertical strips of the batiste and the lace insertion. The skirt is decorated with alternating strips of lace and batiste, and at the very bottom is a ruffle that is gathered and trimmed with the $^{1}/_{4}$-inch lace. The dress opens at the back and closes with three buttons and is 20-inches long. It is circa 1900-1910.

{ *Collection of Ruth and Ralph Fuller, donated by his sister, Elsie Joy, P.O.A., 1992.21.16* }

Golden SILK GOWN

"Each day new trimmings are being opened and so exquisitely beautiful that they take away the every day aspect of dress. Gold and tinsel of every delicate gradation of color play their part, as well as every conceivable tint, so well blended that they cease to individually assert themselves, and yet simply produce one harmonious tone."

—Godey's Lady's Book, "The Fashions. A Monthly Resume of Practical Matters Relating to Dress and Social Events," (June 1881)

Miss Clara Prudence Scott of New Philadelphia, Ohio, wore this golden silk satin afternoon dress about 1895. The two-piece dress, trimmed with metallic passementerie and machine-made blonde lace, whimsically combines historic design elements—the 18th century open robe, stomacher and petticoat. It has a high-standing collar and opens at the center front with hooks and eyes. The two-piece sleeves are the fashionable leg-o'mutton style with an additional triangular piece appliquéd from the shoulder to the elbow to give an extra puff. At each wrist, the sleeves are sewn in decorative points that allow a 5-inch width of machine-made blonde lace to show through. The bust is pleated for added fullness, and the bodice comes to a point at the waist reflecting the pointed stomacher. A 12-inch peplum continues the effect of the open robe by allowing 4-inches of the skirt to be revealed at the center front. The back bodice seaming reflects the robe à l'anglaise of the 1770s. The skirt is decorated at the hem with points over a ruffle of the lace, backed with a pleated flounce and satin banded additional stiffening. The lace is pulled to the surface and tacked at the center of each point.

{ Gift of Robert and Melody Liberatore, 1987.55.2ab }

Bleeding Heart
CHRISTENING GOWN

"She sewed for many a village mite
Its christening-gown of lacy white;
She's sewed—and damped it with a tear—
Its last white frock, uncrumpled, sheer.
She orders what each bride shall wear
With most expert and final air.
Who dares consider foreign aid,
The heresy of "ready-made."
Before her knowing, dauntless mien?
Old, faded, poor, she still is queen."

—*The Youth's Companion*, excerpt "The Village
Seamstress," (January 1910)

As if to insinuate flowers raining down from the heavens pooling at an infant's cherubic feet, the eyelet border fabric on this christening gown becomes more dense with embroidery as it continues down the skirt. It is lovely enough to negate further frills. In total, the gown is 41-inches long. The skirt, together with the eyelet border, is made of dimity stripes used with the warp running crosswise. The bodice and sleeves are made of an eyelet with a more closely spaced pattern. The collar and cuffs are edged with an embroidered and scalloped eyelet edging. The skirt is gathered and sewn to the bodice and has a circumference of 64-inches. The embroidery on the skirt begins 7-inches from the bodice and alternates between lines of small leaves and lines of flowers that look similar to bleeding hearts or freesia.

{ *Gift of J. Jerome Lackamp in memory of Leo G. Lackamp, 1997.70.7* }

Irish Crochet
TODDLER DRESS

"The intention of your being taught needlework, knitting and the like, is not on account of the intrinsic value of all you can do with your hands, which is trifling, but to enable you to judge more perfectly of that kind of work, and to direct the execution of it in others."

— The Christian's Scholar's and Farmer's Magazine, "A Father's Advice to his Daughter," (August 1789)

This sweet little toddler's dress is dated about 1900. The most intriguing aspect of the garment is the Irish crochet bodice. It is an unusual pattern, perhaps created specifically for this piece, as it does somewhat echo the spiral design of the embroidery on the cotton batiste skirt. The dress flaunts the impression of a swirling child in motion partly because of the detailing but also due to the layered, flounced skirt. It has both an under- and over-skirt creating a lovely full, bell appearance. The under layer of the skirt has three ¹/₈-inch hand-stitched tucks right above the lace trim, as well as a 1¹/₈-inch hand-stitched tuck 5-inches above the hem. The skirt's outer layer is white embroidered cotton batiste with a curving floral wreath and lattice pattern. Two different machine-made laces in a *point d'angleterre* style are used at the hem. Two bands of lace join together for the flounce on the underskirt. One is ¹/₂-inch wide and the other 2-inches wide. A comparable lace with a slightly larger pattern is used for the overskirt flounce. The dress has drawstrings at the neck and waist to aid the fit, and an under-bodice joined to the bodice at the waist.

{ Gift of Martha McCaskey Selhorst Collection, 2003.35.2 }

Long-Waisted
TEEN DRESS

"All garment forms are simplifying. They are becoming closer fitting. Sleeve and bodice lines are narrowing. Long pointed effects are coming in. To adapt them to her use the slender woman must study how to apply them to her special requirements, else, having adopted one of the prevailing styles, as adopt them she must, she may fail to be stylish, or even fashionably dressed!"

—*Harper's Bazaar,* "Fashions for Thin Women," (September 1907)

The silhouette, or lack there of, suggests this lace gown was made for a girl in her teen years who was tall, thin and yet to develop. The narrow, elongated bodice pours into a practically non-existent hipline, and the dress was constructed with no darts to accommodate a bustline. The rounded neckline and lace-filled décolletage is quite modest, and just a hint of the upper arm would show through the sheer areas in the sleeves. The embellishment indicates nothing specific; the gown could have been made for any number of occasions—a sweet sixteen party, a cotillion, a wedding garment for the junior bridesmaid, perhaps. The materials, style and construction date the piece between 1908-1912. It has an under layer of silk that has cording sewn into the hem for stiffening. The outer layer of the dress is made from embroidered tulle, chemical lace, square mesh and machine-made lace. The bodice of the garment has short sleeves that are decorated with lace in a lattice pattern with an embroidered flower in each diamond. This treatment continues over the shoulder and covers the back of the bodice. The very bottom of the sleeve is edged with a heavy chemical lace. The neckline is gently rounded below the collarbone and made of five rounds of ¹/₂-inch lace. The midsection of the front bodice utilizes

the square mesh and horizontal insertion between two curved bands of chemical lace. The square mesh is pintucked in a lattice design. The outer layer of the skirt is made from the embroidered tulle with a wide inverted V open at the center front to reveal the under layer of tulle decorated with pintucks and lace appliquéd in a deep zigzag pattern. The top layer also remains open in the back, exposing the underlayer of tulle.

{ *Silverman/Rodgers Collection, 1983.1.246* }

Tiers of Pink
RUFFLES DRESS

" 'I am sweet sixteen, and papa's pet,
Never been kissed by a young man
Yet. Au Revoir
With best wishes from all from
BROWN-EYED PEARL'"

—*Southern Cultivator,* excerpt from a letter
to the editor entitled "Sweet Sixteen and Her
Papa's Pet," (June 1904)

This delightful confection is made from pink silk chiffon, cotton and ribbon trimmed with machine-made lace. It was made around 1905 and would have been a perfect dress for a young lady, perhaps for a sweet sixteen party. Baby-pink layered frills of this nature would have been rather juvenile for a woman of the day, whose fashion sense would have led her to shirtwaist suits or dresses in more decisive lines and colors, or in shades of white (no color at all). The bodice on this frilly dress is pink cotton pintucked in vertical rows down the front—24 pintucks—and back—10 pintucks. It is fully lined with white cotton. The rounded neckline is trimmed with a wide lace. A 6-inch ruffle of pink chiffon trimmed with two rows of $1/4$-inch pink satin ribbon borders the lace at the neck and decorates the pink cotton sleeves. There are hidden hooks and eyes at the center back. The full skirt begins at the waist with a layer of cotton, trimmed vertically in four columns of the same wide lace that fills the décolletage. The skirt is tucked between each strip of lace to tame the fullness into the waistband. The lace travels down the skirt intersecting with more of the same lace, which is applied on top of the first ruffle and dips to wide points. The 10-inch ruffled tiers of the pink cotton are each trimmed with two rows of the pink ribbon.

{ *Silverman/Rodgers Collection, 1983.1.283* }

Floral Vine CHRISTENING GOWN

"There will always be a certain class who will recognize the artistic superiority of hand work and will have no other."

— *The Art Amateur,* "The Future of American Embroidery," (April 1894)

In spite of being made for an infant, this precious silk gown reflects the cut and styling of a woman's gown from the same time, probably about 1770. A piece of this fabrication, quite elaborately embroidered, would have most likely been commissioned by a family of wealth. The side fullness and the pleats stitched down the back to the waist are similar to the fashionable robe à l'anglaise. It is a gorgeous deep cream silk satin christening gown, probably English. It has a tucked and pleated bodice with a full skirt that is embroidered on the front with a scrolling vine and floral pattern. The embroidery continues gracefully around the hem of the garment. The elaborate silk embroidered flowers are worked in long and short, stem, couching and French knots. The tiny sleeves of the dress are embroidered with the same flowers as the skirt and have small cuffs. Delicate straps cover the shoulders and would be stitched or pinned to the bodice fronts. The skirt is 24-inches long.

{ *Silverman/Rodgers Collection, 1983.1.2* }

Embroidered
BIRD BABY DRESS

"The newest cotton embroideries show the combination of lace with embroidery. Some designs show figures of lace let into the embroidered pattern. Medallions of lace and embroidery are very pretty; some of the new ones show a part of the design worked in fillet lace which is rather heavy and has a square mesh."

— *The Ladies' Home Journal*, "The New Spring Trimmings," (April 1907)

A cursory search for birds as they relate to the history of embroidery reveals that they were included among the themes on classical Greek garments as well as one of the various motifs borrowed from nature for use in the embellishment of ancient Chinese attire. Hearts, bows and birds also inspired beautiful works of embroidery and display the craftsmanship of the Victorian seamstress. In her book *Embroidered Birds* (David & Charles Publishers; 2004), author Helen Stevens writes that bird motifs appear throughout history and are second in popularity only to floral designs; ". . . whilst our most ancient ancestors were quick to discover their value as a source of food, it cannot have been long before the decorative and entertainment qualities of birds were also appreciated."

In its intent to look like cutwork, this charming little dress from the early 1900s has lace worked between rectangles of embroidered birds. Here again, the embroidery work is so fetchingly uniform, so indescribably precise, it's hard to fathom each of these intricate and dimensional birds being hand wrought. The bird-and-lace strips are 2-inches wide throughout. The bodice of the dress is made of a center fabric panel of cotton batiste embellished by $^{1}/_{16}$-inch horizontally placed tucks flanked by a section of cutwork embroidery with a scalloped edge. Beyond the cutwork at the shoulders of the bodice is a width of fabric embroidered with a row of birds—the same birds as were worked in the bird-and-lace strips, only this time interspersed with embroidered floral details. The short sleeves are slightly puffed and trimmed with a $^{3}/_{8}$-inch lace that also trims the neckline. The skirt gathers at the waist and 7-inches down is decorated with a pattern of alternating five $^{1}/_{8}$-inch tucks and the bird-and-lace insertion. This repeats two more times so that the dress finishes with the insertion, negating an additional trim or hem.

{ *Gift of Martha McCaskey Selhorst Collection, 2003.35.25* }

Ornamented Wool
TEA GOWN

"Now what are 'tea gowns'? asks a correspondent. They began by being loose but elegant negligees, rather pretty, but not superb. They have become very 'smart' gowns now, as the English say, and many ladies at Nice, Pati, Biarritz, and even in English country houses, wear them at dinner. They are generally Princesse shape and often made of two colors, as brown plush over pink silk front, with crepe or lace falling in front."

—*The Ladies' Home Journal*,*"Afternoon Tea,"* (January 1889)

This tea gown from about 1902 is made of elaborately ornamented cream-colored wool with a very full skirt and a train. It has all the hallmarks of a fashionable tea gown with a variety of decorative elements. The bodice is heavily decorated with chemical lace and has a center back hook-and-eye opening. The sleeves are made of cream tulle with double puffs ending in a tight cuff decorated with four buttons and machine-made point de gaze lace. At the waist and down the front and back of the skirt is a band of larger mesh inset. The mesh is trimmed with cream passementerie in a vine-like pattern. There are cream-colored silk flowers all along the vine as well as the waist and on the yoke of the dress. The flowers have long stems of pleated ribbon. There are also pale yellow silk ribbon flowers here and there on the dress that appear to have been added after the original construction, perhaps as restorations. The train is quite long.

{ *Silverman/Rodgers Collection, 1983.1.289* }

Embroidered Black Velvet
FAUNTLEROY SUIT

"Do not make the mistake of thinking these collars resemble the large overtrimmed collars of the now extinct Little Lord Fauntleroy days because they do not. They are simple in shape, and not over deep, and are worn without the full bow cravat which was a part of the Lord Fauntleroy collar."

—*The Ladies' Home Journal,*"Little Men and Women in the Autumn Clothes," (October 1903)

This little suit, from about 1880, is reminiscent of a Little Lord Fauntleroy suit but without the large white collar and cuffs. Typically, "the nice suits of small boys" were made of "velvet and velveteen" as confirmed in the article, "Fashions for the Little Ones," from *The Cosmopolitan* magazine, (Feb.

1887). Mrs. Helen Hooker, the author, also writes of "soutache embroidery in some simple pattern" as suitable trimming. This suit is embellished with hand embroidery—a floral and leaf design worked in black pearl cotton on the front, back, collar and sleeves, waistband and legs. The jacket is short with long bell sleeves. The length of the outside line of the sleeve is 14-inches long and the jacket from the collar to the waist is 9-inches long. Nine brass buttons hold the jacket closed, and they are set 1-inch apart. The pants button to eight brass buttons on the waistband of the jacket. The buttons are set 3-inches apart. The pants are 19-inches long. The hem of each leg is scalloped and each is decorated on the outside with four tiny brass studs in addition to the embroidery. The pants are fall front and there are pockets on each side. There is also a fly opening in the front of the pants $1^{1}/_{2}$-inches long. There is a tiny half-circle fly flap sewn on the inside behind it.

{ Gift in memory of Constance R. Andrus and Laura Gladys Roosevelt, 1994.48.51ab }

Embroidered
NET DRESS

"In light-weight materials of all kinds it is possible to use very much more fullness in the skirts than in cloth or any of the heavier fabrics and the impossibility of holding up the long skirt of the present moment has been well demonstrated. The skirt that is long in the back and of a reasonable length at the sides can easily be held up in walking, but when it drags at the sides and in front as well as in the back, it is sure to be too cumbersome and clumsy for any woman to hold up comfortably; and for once Fashion has been sensible enough to decree that muddy and dusty skirts are not smart."

—*Harper's Bazaar,* "The Fashion Outlook for Women," (April 1904)

Despite the garden of embroidery that blossoms around the skirt and neckline of this lovely summer dress, what is striking are the gossamer sleeves. They come to just below the elbow, which is particularly telling of the time frame—1906—in which the dress was likely worn. In a *Town and Country*

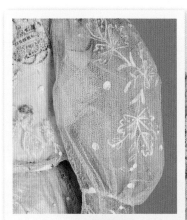

article from the same year, the writer advises that "there is no excuse this season for the swagger, mannish pose or to pull up one's sleeves, the later always giving the effect best expressed by that slang word—meaning, well, not tender." The reader is told that all the gowns have the "coquettish elbow sleeve."

This ideal example of the times is tulle embroidered and appliquéd with flowers, some of heavy chemical lace and others of delicate chain stitch. The bodice has a high-standing collar, and there is an inset of square mesh at the bottom of the yoke and also on the skirt. The aforementioned puffed sleeves are tulle, but more lightly embroidered than the body of gown. The bodice opens at the back from the collar to the top of a 4-inch flower appliqué and closes with five white buttons. The skirt hem has a gathered tulle flounce backing the embroidered tulle, and the cotton satin underskirt has a chiffon flounce to give added body to the full hem.

{ *Silverman/Rodgers Collection, 1983.1.251ab* }

White Cotton and Lace
SUMMER MATINÉE DRESS

"A new feature for the demi-saison and summer toilettes is, that bodices being cut plain and low, are made both full and high by very ornate additional arrangements of surah, lace or velvet; sometimes these separate parts are plastrons, sometimes fichus, sometimes vests, sometimes triple light collars, with corresponding ornaments for the forearms. The summer fabrics are admirably suited for this puffing, draping, and gathering on the shoulders."

—Godey's Lady's Book, "The Fashions. A Monthly Resume of Practical Matters
Relating to Dress and Social Events," (June 1890)

In a July 1899 issue of *Harper's Bazaar* the article "Matinees, Tea Jackets and Negligees," shares that the quaintness of one gown "with its sedate collar and cravat and picturesque sleeve is too pretty to be concealed in one's room." A similar impression is made by this summer morning dress that is virtually dripping with lace. Ample flourishes at the neckline and sleeves create a fullness that is balanced by a generous width at the hem. It is made from white cotton lawn and four machine-made Valencienne laces, two $1/2$-inch edgings, one $3^1/2$-inch edging, and one $2^1/2$-inch lace insertion. The wider laces have the same pattern. The rounded neckline is edged with two $1/2$-inch laces, and the yoke is made from the wide lace insertion. Scalloped lace and lawn ruffles over the bust coming to a point at the center front. The sleeves are covered with four lawn ruffles edged with narrow lace and two wide scalloped lace ruffles. The dress is gently shaped by six rows of shirring at the waist. The skirt has a slight train, and the decoration begins 11-inches from the bottom of the shirring with three alternating strips of 2-inch lace

insertion and folded bias bands of the same width of lawn. A shaped addition of lawn adds length to the back for the train, and two more alternating rows of lace and bias bands continue to increase the width of the skirt forming almost a complete circle about 23-feet in circumference. The hem of the skirt is completed with a strip of the wider lace insertion joined to the scalloped edge lace and backed by a lawn ruffle. The dress opens in the back and closes with six lace-covered buttons at the top and hook-and-eye closures down to about 7-inches below the waist. The dress may have been worn simply loose and flowing or with a ribbon tie at the waist.

{ Silverman/Rodgers Collection, 1983.1.2148 }

Ivory Net
TEA DRESS

"Her tiny ears are covered
With her hair of golden brown.
Her swan-like neck is open
To the gaze of half the town;
Her ankles, trim and graceful,
That delight the roving eye,
With a filmy gauze are covered
That intrigues the passer-by."

—*Life*, excerpt from "The Flapper,"
(December 1920)

An elongated silhouette with a slightly flaired hemline fits comfortably into the category of 1920s costume, yet this heirloom version is somewhat more demure than the reputation implied by the flapper era. It is made of ivory tulle and lace, perfect for afternoon tea with friends. It would have been worn in the mid 1920s over a simple slip, the most obvious departures from the previous decade being its sleeveless style and shorter hemline. The neckline is square and trimmed with a simple $^1/_4$-inch fold-over of tulle whipped to the lace outline. The front and the back are the same except that the neckline in the back is slightly higher. The center of both sides has a 5-inch wide vertical tulle panel machine embroidered in a heavy floral pattern. The panel is framed on each side by two $1^1/_2$-inch wide strips of machine-made lace that have a floral motif on a bar ground. These joined lace strips continue to the hem but split to accommodate tulle godets trimmed with four curves of $^5/_8$-inch lace insertion joined to tulle ruffles. The sides of the garment are made of tulle with woven stripes that resemble narrow tucks.

{ *Gift of Rebecca Burton, 1984.25.2* }

Wild Rose
WHITE PIQUÉ COAT

"The piqué coat has become a recognized part of the wardrobe of a child. Made in piqué or duck, it has the look of dressiness as well as utility, and the same model will serve equally well for flannel or heavier cloth."

—*Pictorial Review*, "For Children's Wear," (June 1900)

"Fine ribbed piqué is always in vogue for children's short clothes. The little piqué coats are particularly pretty finished with scalloped edges and buttonholed." This, from "Mrs. Ralston's Chat About Children's Clothes," couldn't be a more fitting description of this little coat. While Mrs. Ralston's take on children's fashions was from the July 1906 edition of *Ladies' Home Journal*, this coat is dated slightly earlier due to the leg-o' mutton sleeves.

This 1890s piqué coat is quite charming. It is embroidered with a climbing wild rose pattern that adorns the collar edge, the cuffs, the front hemline, and the center front opening. The handwork is a combination of open roses and rosebuds in satin stitch and French knots. All the edges of the coat are scalloped and finished with a satin and featherstitch design. The collar is a wide sailor design, and the sleeves are leg-o'mutton and are pleated at the cuff line and shoulder. The cuff is a separate piece of piqué, embellished and sewn to the sleeve. The four pleats that gather in the fullness of the sleeve cap are 1-inch box pleats. Each of the five traditional pleats on the sleeves is stitched down with a double row of machine stitching. The sailor collar comes to points in the front and is squared off in back. The coat attaches with one large white button at the base of the collar.

{ *Gift of Daniel Jonas in memory of Helene Brill Jonas, 1989.26.38* }

Ribbon-Striped DIMITY & LACE DRESS

"The long effect in line given by the one-piece dresses is undoubtedly a most becoming style for many children, and this reason is no doubt responsible for their popularity."

—*The Ladies' Home Journal*, "Little Men and women in their Autumn Clothes," (Oct. 1903)

Children's pieces can be such a mystery. Imagine a historian in the future trying to date a dropped-waist heirloom dress made with French sewing techniques and antique laces. The style might be completely early 20th century, the lace might be older, yet construction and fabric quality suggests something much more current. This little dress falls into that category. The style places it anywhere from the early 1900s, due to the dropped waist and high neck, to as late as the 30s, evidenced by the elongated silhouette. The nature of the construction, both machine and

hand, indicates it may have been made towards the latter part of the first quarter, as does the dimity fabric. One definite is that its origin is Ohio.

This dress is made from creamy ribbon-striped cotton dimity with machine-made lace insertion. It closes in the center back with six buttons from the collar to the waist. It is both machine and hand stitched and was most likely made at home as the stitching lines are not straight nor are they uniform. There are no raw edges under the lace inserts, as they were machine and hand finished (all raw edges of the cut and folded back fabric, turned under and secured by hand or machine). Each lace insert is $3/4$-inch wide, and each woven stripe in the voile is $1/4$-inch wide. The skirt is gathered from the right front hip around the back to the left front hip. The hem is 3-inches wide. A straight panel remains down the middle of the dress and creates an elongated line. The neckline is turned under and finished with a narrow hem to which a collar of mitered lace insertion, a $1/8$-inch fabric band and a lace edging is applied. The slightly puffed sleeves are finished with a bias band topped and hidden by a trim of lace insertion joined to very slightly gathered lace edging.

{ *Gift in memory of Jennie Griteman, 1992.3.1* }

Butterfly Sleeves DRESS

"We cannot too strongly advise the novice to take the precaution of cutting and fitting a model of muslin or crinoline, not only of the new sleeves but of every pattern that is cut on new and unfamiliar lines. The acquaintance this gives with the work will more than repay for the extra time and trouble."

—*Pictorial Review*, "A Chapter on Sleeves," (March 1904)

"Of all dressmaking problems, the sleeve is perhaps the most perplexing that presents itself to the home dressmaker today, for upon its shape and trimming often depends the entire success of the garments." This, from "A Chapter on Sleeves" from the March 1904 edition of *Pictorial Review* has proven all too true on this charming child's dress from the same time period. The butterfly sleeve is what first draws the eye and what sets the dress apart from a typical round yoke design. It is from the late 19th century and full of intricate details and frills, but the sleeves are, by far, the most interesting aspect. The upper sleeves are made of two pieces of fabric gathered into a double puff separated by a strip of the whitework insertion giving the illusion of a butterfly. The lower sleeves are slightly full and end in a narrow band of featherstitch embroidery and 1¼-inch bobbin lace, joined to a gathered and scalloped bobbin lace edging. The bodice of the dress is made from alternating vertical strips of lace and embroidered insertion. The center of the yoke is made of alternating strips of 1½-inch eyelet and 1¼-inch bobbin lace both front and back, with featherstitching at the joins and around the neckband, and with the remaining fabric of the yoke covered with rows of featherstitching. The skirt of the dress is gathered to the yoke below a flounce of scalloped bobbin lace

that outlines the entire yoke. Beginning 7-inches from the yoke are 22 tucks each ¼-inch wide and spaced ⅛-inch apart. This joins a horizontal panel 5¼-inches wide pieced with vertical lace and whitework and diagonal strips of whitework, with the fabric in between covered with featherstitching. All the joined edges are sewn under and decorated with featherstitching. A strip of the lace, a strip of the whitework and a strip of wider scalloped lace finish the hem. The dress is 28-inches long. It closes at the center back with three buttons and a fabric drawstring at the neck.

{ Gift of Martha McCaskey Selhorst Collection, 2003.35.30 }

Neo-Classic Greek Key
AYRSHIRE CHRISTENING GOWN

"The early stitchers were referred to as 'flowerers' because of the flower motifs they created."

—The Sharp Needle "Ayrshire Embroidery," (2002 Beth Gardner)

It's difficult to comprehend a lady embroidering such an intricate and virtually symmetrical motif of this magnitude when she would have worked by light of day or poor candle glow. Hours of effort went into skillfully embroidering the skirt front, and filling in the front yoke in the form of created insertions joined by entredeux edge and interspersed with fabric godets topped with featherstitch. A Scottish technique that thrived in Glascow, Ayrshire embroidery offered a way for poor farm women to supplement their income. A family would have cherished this gown, passing it down through the generations, although no documentation is available to prove such an assertion.

The christening gown is of classic Ayrshire whitework embroidery worked on delicate white cotton mull. Stalks of wheat and daisy-like flowers are intertwined with a neo-Classic Greek key design winding down the center front of the gown in a graduated pattern. This wonderful, symmetrical embroidery is worked in satin stitch, French knots, featherstitch, and drawn thread embroidery. The bodice has slightly puffed sleeves, which finish with a 1/4-inch binding and an ever so slightly gathered lace edging. The same binding and lace treatment finishes the neckline, and a drawstring run through the binding serves to fit and secure the gown at the back opening. A loop and fabric-covered button, positioned at the bottom of the yoke where it joins the skirt, fastens the gown in back. The gown was probably made in the first decade of the 19th century.

{ Silverman/Rodgers Collection, 1983.1.54 }

Ruffled Chantilly
LACE DRESS

"What viewers-with-alarm forget is, that while the knees are coming out the neck is going in. Woman has merely moved her clothes up a few inches. Presently, without doubt, she will move them back down again, and there will be a fresh outburst of denunciation from the chronic objectors. Not however from those who bear in mind the principle of varying disclosure."

— *The Independent*, "Fashions and the Female," (Feburary 1926)

Once the boyish flapper look of the 1920s ran its course, the '30s ushered in an alluring, feminine approach to dressing. Both necklines and hemlines dropped. Silhouettes followed a woman's curves more closely. Ruffles and tiers re-emerged in stunning fashion. This flirty dancing dress from about 1935 is an exquisite example, made of horizontal rows of 2-inch wide machine-made chantilly lace in peach and ecru. The laces, matching insertion and edging are applied to a tulle foundation. A bright pink silk lining shows through the lace and tulle and gives extra depth to the color. The neckline in front and back is a V, formed from a mitered placement of the wide chantilly insertion. A horizontal placement of insertion fills in the shoulder area. From the bust to the hip, two gathered bands of scalloped peach edging alternate with a band of insertion lace. From the hip to the hem, the dress is covered with gathered rows of the scalloped peach lace edging. All of the lace is straight stitched onto the tulle body. Between the tulle and the lining, positioned six ruffles from the bottom is a 2-inch strip of horsehair interfacing, applied presumably to give the skirt a touch of body and keep it from entangling between the legs. The bodice of the dress is sleeveless, and both the armscye and the neckline are finished with the tiniest band of tulle, rolled tightly enough to insinuate a tulle piping. A side opening under the left arm closes with 12 snaps. Peach and pale blue-green velvet ribbons encircle the waist and form a bow at the left side.

{ *Gift of Evangeline Davey Smith, (Mrs. Alexander M. Smith) in memory of Mrs. Martin L. Davey, Sr. (Bernice Chrisman Davey), 1991.11.177* }

Bleeding Heart Blossoms
EMBROIDERY BLOUSE

"The hand-embroidered blouses that have taken the place of shirt waists and that form the chief coquetries of the tailor-made girls are shown in many new designs by Miss Martha. One dear little blouse has a design in thistle buds while on another wild roses with the stems starting at the waist spread out to the yoke above, with the full blown blossoms cleverly designed and embroidered. In these blouses, women make use of the best laces of all nations."

— Town and Country, "Coquetries of Home; Linens Laces and Blue-Ribbon Bows," (April 1905)

A strong sense of romance plays into the design of this embroidered "waist." It draws its charm from the beautifully embroidered bleeding heart blossoms, which flourish about the yoke and sleeves, pairing sweetly with a floral lace. It's a lovely silk piece, typical of the waists of the first few years of the 20th century. The collar and yoke are made up of strips of lace insertion. The bleeding heart blossoms and leaves are embroidered in a heavy silk twist. An additional inset of machine-made mesh is stitched in scallops interspersed with the embroidery. The bodice is gathered into a band at the waist and has a short peplum varying in depth from 3- to 5-inches, to tuck into the skirt. The elbow-length sleeves are decorated at the cuffs with rows of gathered lace, and the sleeves themselves have lace insertion edged with gathered lace in a curving pattern that surrounds an embroidered central motif similar to the design on the front. The design of the sleeve embroidery is also found on both sides of the center back.

{ *Gift of Barbara D. Gundaker in memory of Anna K. Gundaker, 1993.46.6* }

Circle of Tulle
DRESS

"During the 19th century child labor laws and social welfare programs began to remedy the numerous wrongs inflicted on children, but the next great social change did not occur until the 20th century when the First World War triggered a relaxation of manners and simplification of dress for all age groups."

—"Centuries of Childhood" Kent State University Museum, Anne Bissonnette, Curator
(September 2000)

The simplest approach is so often the most endearing. This fine pink overlay, dotted with yarn blossoms, is but a fabric circle. It might have been purchased as part of a portrait ensemble—the toddler would have worn a slip or dress underneath—to picture-perfectly frame baby's precious face and rest gently over her shoulders.

The pale pink tulle is a seamless circle with an opening cut at the center to accommodate what little structure exists—that of the neckband. It is made from two arcs of an oval that form the sleeves as well. The diameter of the large circle is 32-inches, and the center cut out is 9-inches. The dress is decorated with yarn embroidery in soft pastels of pink, yellow and blue. There is a small label in the dress that reads "Made in Italy, Size 2." The dress dates from the 1930s.

{ *Gift of Mrs. Harry McDonald, 1986.103.143* }

Ecru Silk Dress
WITH LACE SWIRLS & FABRIC ROSES

"The lines of the gown were simple, but the elaboration in trimming, applications (there were also lace medallions) and embroidery were intricate beyond description in words."

—Town and Country, "Springtime Modes and Colors," (March 1906)

Identified as one of "Miss Clark's Gowns," this model has a garden of fabric roses placed about the bodice, the sleeves and trellising up the skirt. Perhaps the dressmaker's client tended her own roses, blossoms of every hue that sent fragrance indoors on the summer breezes, or maybe she took pride in the art of arranging stems in vases to fill her home with splashes of color. A decade prior, the *Saturday Evening Post* noted that "some ladies now wear, fastened to their waist a bunch of roses or some other tied with a ribbon. It has a pretty effect, and looks simple, but the flowers quickly fade in that position as they come in contact with the wearer's arms and with the table, and do not long keep their fresh appearance." Mrs. Clark's silk roses have retained their beauty for a century, save for needing to be "fluffed."

This dress, which dates from about 1907, is a delicate plain-weave silk, and the inside label reads "Miss Clark Gowns Philadelphia Pa." It has a high-standing collar made from appliquéd lace that forms a shallow yoke at the center front. The work surrounding the yoke is quite complicated. First is a silk band, piped and scalloped along the inner edge and applied in a V shape then topped with two-tone embroidered leaves and self-fabric silk rosettes. This work is followed by an embroidered, machine-made netting lace of a dense swirl design. The lace is extremely delicate

throughout. Both the silk band and the netting lace continue over the shoulders and into the back waistband. A loose drape of gathered silk, again embellished with rosettes and two-tone embroidered leaves, combines with a drape of netting lace to complete the lower section of the bodice and establish a pouter-pigeon silhouette. Here, the larger rosettes are decorated with embroidered details. The back yoke of the dress is the same lace fill as the front. The gathered silk waist sash is hidden in front by the lace drape, but in back it fastens under a 5-inch braided band of silk with a bow at each end. The three-quarter length sleeves are made of the netting lace, and each is decorated mid-sleeve and at the cuff with a strip of the silk; a rosette is added at mid-sleeve. The skirt of the garment has a panel down the front that is framed on either side by strips of the netting swirl lace. The sides and back of the skirt are elegantly decorated about three-quarters of the way down with three rows of a silk passementarie and a deep tuck topped with a trellis of embroidered leaves and large rosettes. The dress has a slight train embellished from the center panel with a strip of netting lace.

The dress opens up the back and fastens with hook and eye closures. There is also an attached silk petticoat with two rows of ruffles at the hem, possibly a replacement, judging by its condition.

{ Silverman/Rodgers Collection, 1983.1.240 }

Crepe Dress
WITH BLUE SMOCKING

"Smocking is also a favorite form of trimming children's frocks."
—*The American Farmer,* "Fashions Fangies," (December 1893)

Smocking was noted as a "favorite form of trimming for children's frocks" in *The American Farmer* (Dec. 1893). It has been an integral way of decoratively manipulating fabric fullness for centuries prior and has remained as a classic treatment on children's apparel and some adult fashions into the 21st century. This dress was worn by Barbara Helen Lee Loomis probably between 1925 and 1930 when she was about 5 years old. The piece is in fine condition, and may have been worn only on occasions during which it wasn't likely to get soiled, as it is made from white silk crepe. The embellishments are generous and precisely placed, the most notable of which is the smocking. It is pale blue and decorates the shoulders, cuffs, pocket and three panels on the upper back. The effect of the smocking at the shoulders is to create a faux yoke. The smocking design is the same throughout—a single step, mirror-imaged trellis creating a series of diamonds. On the pocket, the design is worked in such a way that it forms an inverted triangle over very loosely pleated fabric. The dress is 28-inches long and 42-inches in circumference. It slips over the head and has a slit down the front that closes with four toggle buttons that are inserted through round embroidered buttonholes. The buttons are made from bias tubes knotted at both ends. The buttons and the points of the collar are decorated with French knots. The hem is hand sewn and is decorated right above the seam with a line of featherstitching. A tiny yoke that measures 22-inches wide at the neckline and 1-inch wide at the sleeve seam joins the front and back of the dress at the shoulders. The collar appears to have been applied by hand, and the interior seam is covered with seam tape. A 3-inch long piece of $1/8$-inch wide tape was hand tacked to the center of the neckline on top of the seam tape presumably to hang the dress on a hook. The remainder of the seams on the garment are machine sewn.

{ *Gift of Barbara A. Tyler, 1987.8.1a-e* }

Rickrack
BIRTHDAY PARTY DRESS

"All their dresses, however, are made in one piece until they are 16, when they are promoted to the dignity of separate skirts and bodices. Until they are eight or nine years old their frocks hang simply from a yoke. Between nine and 16 their bodices and skirt pieces are sewed together at the waistline, with either a cord, piping or narrow girdle to conceal the joining."

—*The American Farmer*, "Fashions Fangies," (December 1993)

This charming two-piece dress was made for little Henrietta Wick's eighth birthday in 1884. That historical tidbit came with the garment when it became part of the Kent State Museum Collections; nothing more is certain. It can be assumed that a dear relative carefully made the dress in the months leading up to the event, and that the child wore the special dress to receive her party guests. The skirt is made from white broadcloth gathered at the waist. There are buttonholes at each side and at the center front and back that would button to both the bodice and an undergarment. The skirt is 21-inches long and has two alternating bands of horizontal tucking and lace. The top row of tucks has seven $^1/_4$-inch tucks that are $^1/_8$-inch apart; stitching marks indicate that there was once an eighth tuck, let out, presumably as Henrietta grew. The bottom row has eight $^1/_8$-inch tucks that are $^1/_8$-inch apart. The rickrack lace was popular during the late 19th century and early 20th century when tape laces were widely used. It is made by crocheting the rickrack into shapes. The bands of lace on the skirt are 2- and 4-inches wide. The bodice is also made from white broadcloth and the same lace as the skirt. The lace neck yoke extends down the outside of the three-quarter sleeves. It has a high neck, constructed of a fabric band, and opens in the back where five buttons would have closed it. The under-sleeves are made from two pieces of cloth.

{ *Gift of Bernice J. Wicks, 1988.51.5ab* }

Champagne
BRIDESMAID'S DRESS

"Simplicity, ever the key note of good taste in dress, is particularly desirable in the gowns worn at either a church or home wedding."

—*Ladies' Home Journal,* "The Easter Bride and her Bridesmaids," (March 1901)

Despite appeals for "simplicity" in special occasion dress of the early 1900s, many gowns rivaled today's bridal fare in both design approach and embellishment. Original designs and drawings by Katherine Vaughan Holden in a spring edition of *Ladies' Home Journal* lavished period brides and their attendants in lace, fabric flowers, and shirring.

This particular bridesmaid's dress, labeled A. E. Ross, 734 Nth 20th St., Philadelphia, was worn in 1905 and is quite similar to Ms. Holden's interpretations. It is a soft and creamy silk taffeta decorated with appliquéd lace and self-fabric flowers. The bodice has a 3-inch standing collar of the lace, a shirred chiffon yoke with a wide ruffle of lace at the bottom edge and eight $1^1/_2$-inch wide silk rosettes spaced evenly around the garment. The bodice has puffed sleeves with a lace flounce at the elbow. The fullness is controlled at the inside arm by four rows of gathered tucks. The bodice opens all the way down the back and fastens with hooks and eyes. The back of the bodice has a section of ruffled tucks directly under the yoke. The waistband of the bodice is made from a gathered strip of the silk that comes to a point in the front and has two rosettes at the center back. The simple but graceful skirt has a 7-inch wide pleated panel down the front and a gathered panel down the back. There are gathered tucks at each hip, front and back, at each knee in the front and slightly above each knee in the back. The hemline is made from three $1^1/_2$-inch tucks.

{ *Transferred from the Allen Memorial Art Museum, Oberlin College, Oberlin, Ohio. Gift of Gladys Sellew, 1958, 1995.17.96* }

Vertical Tucks & Broderie
ANGLAISE DRESS

"The outfitting and clothing of children for the country, which once occupied matters so exclusively that they had little time left for other duties at this season of the year, is now greatly simplified and rendered a pleasing duty by Messrs. Bes & Co, Liliputian Bazar. Each and every article worn by boys, girl, and babies can here be selected from a larger and better assortment than can be found elsewhere and at surprisingly low prices."

—*Christian Union*, "Children's Clothing," (June 1885)

The image of a child who wore this dress is one of ringlets and button-up ankle shoes. She's carrying a china doll or pretending to take tea. This would have been a favorite dressy dress, because of the waves of open embroidery that appear to be in constant motion lending a sense of movement to the dress even when the child is still. She would have never suspected the effort that went into making the virtually perfect hand-worked eyelet. So uniform and impeccably wrought, the hours of devotion are beyond comprehension.

The cotton dress, most likely from the 1880s is a charming classic with its alternating bands of tucking and hand-worked eyelet insertion. It is machine sewn with both vertical and horizontal hand tucks. The front and back each have four bands of seven $^1/_8$-inch tucks. Each band is 2-inches wide and is separated by a $1^1/_2$-inch wide band of eyelet insertion. The insertion, in a *broderie anglaise* style, has a design of wavy lines, leaves and stars. This insertion is also found around the waist and each sleeve near the cuff. The collar and cuffs are decorated with a different eyelet insertion 1-inch wide. The shoulder seams are covered with a $^1/_4$-inch strip of muslin on the outside, as are the joins between the sleeve and the eyelet cuff and the eyelet cuff and the embroidered edging. The skirt of the garment has a band of five $^1/_4$-inch wide pleats and is trimmed with a 1-inch wide eyelet insertion that has a scalloped edge. The garment opens all the way down the back and is fastened with seven buttons from the collar to the top of the skirt. The bodice is not finished on the inside.

{ *Silverman/Rodgers Collection, 1983.1.215* }

Filet Lace
HEIRLOOM PEIGNOIR

"The lady herself wore a peignoir trimmed with the most exquisite English point. Never had she looked more lovely."

—*Harper's Bazaar*, "Cobwebs of Fashion," (September, 1879)

A lady's boudoir apparel circa 1910 would have been fashioned with the same elegant hand and attention to detail as all the pieces in her wardrobe, but unlike her day and evening gowns that gave little or no thought to comfort, nightclothes were flowing and loose fitting so she could spend at least her sleeping hours unencumbered. This lovely peignoir (or dressing gown) is made from soft white cotton and lace. The cotton is hand embroidered with single roses and roses on stems. The embroidery is primarily done with satin stitch, tiny French knots and some pulled-thread work. Bands of 4^1/$_2$-inch wide insertion made of machine-made filet lace make a triangular collar with ends that hang down in the front, and the same insertion is used to define the bodice and to decorate the sleeves. A pointed 1-inch filet lace border edges the sleeves, center fronts and hem. The skirt of the garment is slightly gathered. The sleeves have pointed tippets and are open in the front from the elbow down.

{ Gift of Elaine Burrell in memory of Myrtle Barrows, 1996.36.2 }

Sleeveless Angled YOKE PINAFORE

"It is now the fashion to make little girls' dresses so that they may leave the neck and arms bare . . ."

—*Pictorial Review,* "For Children's Wear," (June 1900)

As the 20th century headed into its teens, the trend was to push the waistline up to its more natural positioning. Typically, fullness would have been gathered in by a sash, a belt or a button waistband. This little pinafore combines a sash tied in back with an eyelet front waistband. The band bridges the ruched bodice to the gathered skirt. The sashes are sufficiently long to tie into an adequate bow and are sewn to the pinafore in the front at the ends of the eyelet waistband. The pinafore is made from white cotton batiste. The full length of the garment is 21-inches, and each sleeve opening is $4^1/_2$-inches long. The yoke of the pinafore is made of hand-worked eyelet in a geometric pattern placed at opposing angles to create a V neckline; the ruffles at the armscye are made of floral eyelet $1^1/_2$-inches wide that also decorates the ends of the sashes. The band at the waist is a third eyelet. The pinafore opens all the way down the back and closes with three top buttons that are metal covered with fabric. The skirt is decorated near the hem with four tucks that are each $^1/_2$-inch wide and $^1/_2$-inch apart. The sashes have three tucks above the lace edging.

{ *Gift of David and Martha Sinkler in memory of Mary Sinkler, 1992.41.4* }

Vertical Stripes
OF PUFFING DRESS

"The most striking features in children's styles this season is the closeness with which they follow the styles of their elders. The little girls wear berthas ad bretelles, epaulets, and revers, puffs and ruches with the same lavishness as their mammas."

—The American Farmer, "What the Little Folks Wear," (December 1893)

Suddenly in current-day fashion, the use of puffing abounds, around necklines, hemlines, as sleeve treatments and waistbands, yet in fashion, as in sewing, nothing is new. Gathering strips of fabric, called "puffing" in heirloom sewing circles, is an age-old embellishment technique. In this child's example, strips are alternated with two different bobbin laces comprising the entire dropped waist bodice and sleeves. It is modeled with the same lace and puffing detail as an adult afternoon gown of the 1880s. The bobbin lace of the bodice is 1¹/₂-inches wide and worked in a pattern of diamonds and pinwheel shapes. The puffing strips are 2-inches wide. The lace at the cuffs, collar and on the hem double flounce is 2-inches wide and has a flower pattern with a scalloped edge. On the edges of the strips of puffing are narrow fabric bands for reinforcement and each strip is hand sewn to the lace at the edge. The collar of the dress is finished with a bias band and opens at the center back. The dress opens all the way down and has five buttons from the collar to the top of the horizontal lace flounces. The buttons are hidden on the inside left and attach through the right side. The back is no different from the front with the exception of the opening at the center back collar and a hint of a placket where the skirt joins the bodice.

{ Transferred from the Allen Memorial Art Museum, Oberlin College, Oberlin, Ohio. Gift of the estate of Margaret Morfoot through Mrs. Robert Wheeler, 1973, 1995.17.745 }

White Dotted Net and Lace
SUMMER LINGERIE DRESS & SHAWL

"Ruffled sleeves, airy and gossamer in texture, conceal, because they harmonize with the thin arm; whereas thick ruffles cause such a member to appear pipe-stemish as it emerges from them."

—Harper's Bazaar, "Fashions for Thin Women," (September 1907)

The cascading ruffles of dotted net poured over the shoulder, down the sleeves and into the skirt give this gown a sense of fluidity and movement. A shawl completes the ensemble and is coordinated with the gown down to its geometric embroidery and ruffled detail. Together the pieces insinuate a summer calendar filled with social teas and afternoon gatherings. The ensemble dates from about 1912 and is made from white machine-made *point d'esprit*, embroidered tulle insertion and scalloped lace edging. The rounded neckline is trimmed with 1^1/$_2$-inch embroidered lace insertion and two layers of ruffled net trimmed with lace; the insertions have a geometric pattern. The bodice is a full silhouette that ends at the waist with a strip of the embroidered insertion. The elbow-length sleeves have alternating sections of pintucked *point d'esprit*, embroidered insertion and ruffles of *point d'esprit* edged in lace. The skirt fits smoothly over the hips with three horizontal pintucks below the waistband as decoration. The dress has a slight train, and the hem is decorated with bands of embroidered insertion, *point d'esprit* ruffles, pintucked *point d'esprit*, five ^{1}/$_2$-inch tucks separated by ^{5}/$_8$-inch, and a final lace-edged *point d'esprit* ruffle. The dress has a separate shawl that is worn over the shoulders. It is 55-inches long and made from two contoured pieces of point d'esprit with a seam down the middle. The whole is framed with the embroidered insertion and then trimmed with a 2-inch ruffle of *point d'esprit* and lace edging.

{ Gift of Martha McCaskey Selhorst, 1996.58.3ab }

Velvet-Trimmed DRESS COAT

"Leg-of-mutton sleeves, or high velvet puffs around the neck and armholes are seen on the Normandy overcoats worn by very young children for an outside wrap."

—*The Cosmopolitan,* "Fashions for Little Ones," (February 1887)

oats have evolved in such a way that any variety made from wool or a non-waterproof fabrication would be considered a dress coat today, elegant and classic, but non-essential apparel. In the 19th century, coats were nearly as decorative as the garments worn beneath, and they were a necessary part of

a child's wardrobe. Cooler climates required seasonal styles—lightweight for spring perhaps in piqué, silk, muslin or linen, and heavier coats in wool, broadcloth or velvet for winter, trimmed in furs and braids. *Arthur's Home Magazine*, Feb. 1869, cites white knitted jackets worn close up to the neck and down to the wrists; "the most useful and serviceable things, and no child's wardrobe is complete without them."

This charming little coat is made from heavy grey wool and lined with black cotton satin. It is 24-inches long from the collar to the hem and is very full. It closes with three buttons under the collar at the center front. The yoke is embellished with two gathered wool ruffles that go over the full sleeves. The collar, the yolk, the ruffles, and the cuffs are all trimmed at the edges with three rows of $^3/_{16}$-inch black velvet ribbon. The sleeves are puffed in a leg-o'mutton style. This coat was bought and worn in Cleveland, Ohio, about 1895.

{ *Gift of Cowan O'Neil in memory of the Britton-Koykka Family, 1986.112.21* }

Basic Yoke Dress
WITH GOLD BUTTONS

"Children's clothing should be watched even more carefully than that of grown persons, lest it get beyond repair; one day's wear, or merely one romping frolic, after a hole has started, will sometimes completely destroy a garment; and you will need to use as much care in mending as for your own, for they are observant of such matters, and are often more mortified by a patch being made too apparent than by wearing the dress in rags."

—*The New England Farmer,* "Ladies' Department," (August 1868)

This little dress is a simple but lovely basic yoke design—a precursor to the French sewing classics that heirloom enthusiasts reproduce today. The fabric of the skirt is made from alternating strips of lace and insertion approximately 6-inches wide. The same lace and insertion pattern fills the yoke of the dress. The sleeves are puffed and finished with 2-inches of the alternating lace bands like the skirt. The back of the dress is held together by tiny gold buttons that are similar to studs. Each one is engraved with the letter "k," perhaps the child's name was Kathlene or Katrina. Each button is joined to the next by a short length of gold chain.

{ *Gift of Barbara D. Gundaker in memory of Anna K. Gundaker, 1993.46.15* }

Delicate Blue Flowers
AFTERNOON DRESS

"Practically all women of the home today are needlewomen. All the popular embroidery, all the fashionable stitches, are long, padded and quickly worked."

—*Harper's Bazaar*, "Economy in Wash Gowns," (May 1909)

This charming, two-piece ensemble is made of white cotton batiste embroidered with individual blue flowers and garlands of blue flowers and leaves. It would have served as the perfect summer afternoon dress in the early 20th century—a dress for strolling through the park or perhaps watching a game of croquet. The blouse has a standing collar of rows of $^3/_8$-inch lace insertion alternating with $^1/_4$-inch rows of white lace tape. The tape is layered over the headings of the insertions and straight stitched. The shallow yoke is made of shaped lace and lace tape fashioned with darts and godets in such a way that it resembles a cobweb at center front. The lace yoke is mitered and squared off at the shoulder line, which appears to drop slightly to the back of the gown. Opposing angles of the square are topped with a single embroidered flower. Beyond the yoke are 35 vertical pintucks along the shoulders and across the front that manage the fullness and come to a point at the center front. A garland of blue flowers is embroidered on top of the upper portion of the pintucks following the curve of the front yoke. The sleeves of the blouse are slightly full and reach to the elbow with a 3-inch lace flounce that drapes gracefully just below the elbow; the flounce alternates three strips of insertion with two strips of lace tape, ending in two strips of very slightly gathered and overlapped edging. The body of the blouse and the sleeves are sprinkled with the blue satin-stitched flowers. The blouse is held together in the back by 15 small cloth-covered buttons. The top three buttons in back on the standing collar are covered by small bows made of gathered satin and lace—this pretty detail would have rested just under a Gibson Girl, up-swept hairstyle. The skirt consists of five petal-shaped panels outlined and joined by lace tape and insertion trim. Each panel is slightly gathered into the waistband with six pintucks. Six pintucks are also centered beneath the join of each petal on the lower section of the skirt. Each panel's embroidery is identical—three offset flowers tumbling into an embroidered garland. The skirt fastens at a side placket worked between two of the panels; it closes with yokes and tiny chain-stitched eyes. The lower section or flounce of the skirt is pieced together in three sections to achieve the desired fullness. It is finished with four $^1/_4$-inch tucks placed a scant inch apart and a strip of the insertion and lace-tape trim, stitched in such a way that it incorporates the $2^1/_2$-inch hem.

{ *Gift of Martha McCaskey Selhorst, 1996.58.209* }

Latticework
BABY BUBBLE

"A single yard of material is required for this new and practical over-all romper. For real out-of-doors play it should be made of dark serviceable material. For less strenuous requirement, it could be made of white or light-colored poplin."

—*The Modern Priscilla*, "A Play Garment for Little Tots," (March 1918)

The adorable latticework alone makes this blue-green cotton romper a favored piece of the children's collection at The Kent State Museum. The vintage design would draw as many compliments today as it would have at the time of its original wearing, which is estimated to be around 1930.

Modern constraints, however, would dictate the tie at the neck be significantly shorter, or perhaps replaced by a loop and button. The romper is 17½-inches from the neck to the crotch and 32-inches in circumference. It opens and closes at the crotch with two buttons. Two front pockets are decorated with latticework. Each pocket is 4-inches wide and 3-inches long. There is a center front keyhole opening that closes with long ties that are trimmed with tassel ends. The same latticework that is on the pockets can be found at each shoulder. The lattice crossings are held together with tiny cross-stitches made of thread that is the same color as the romper. Bias binding trims the neckline, the keyhole opening and the sleeveless edges. There is also a self-belt that is sewn on the left side of the left pocket, comes around the back and snaps at the right side of the right pocket. The romper dates from about 1930.

{ Gift of Frances Chase Courtsal in memory of the Chase and Tonkinson Families, 1994.29.14 }

Raspberry Silk EVENING DRESS

"We may however, point out that there is, in the matter of dress proper, a decided feeling in favor of the simplicity of bygone days; we mean simplicity as applied to the arrangement of material only, for the richness and variety of the fabrics now produced—silk, satins, and brocades—coupled with their magnificent coloring and beauty of design, preclude all pretension to the use of the term on the score of economy or even moderate price."

—Saturday Evening Post, "Ladies' Department, Fashion Chat," (January 1884)

Created in the early 1820s, at the beginning of the Romantic period of fashion, this lovely raspberry silk dress looks like a bright blossom with layers of petals at the skirt hem. Each petal is gathered and attached to the dress under softly padded rouleaux. From point to rouleaux, each petal is $5^{1}/_{2}$-inches long. The dress has an empire waistline with gathers on the bodice at both front and back. The short capelet sleeves, which continue in front and back at an angle into the waistband, have a layer of silk petals over a puff of white net trimmed with raspberry silk sleeve bands and matching thread buttons. Tiny embroidered balls hang from the buttons like tassels. The neckline has a drawstring closure at the center back, and there is a raspberry silk ribbon at the waist that passes through an opening in the right side of the waistband to tie in the front. The dress has a pocket on the right hip and is lined with white cotton. Just imagine the embroidered handkerchief it might have held.

{ *Gift of Colin Lawton Johnson, 2002.35.6* }

Shark's Tooth CHRISTENING GOWN

"She never had a dress yet—from her christening gown, that I worked myself at odd hours, for a whole year, to that white one she is sitting there at the window making for her wedding—but we have earned with the labor of our hands."

—*Littell's Living,* "Annie Orme," (November 1852)

The precision of shark's teeth makes it one of the more intriguing forms of fabric manipulation, and it is the sole embellishment on the skirt of this simple christening gown, perhaps sparingly trimmed for a baby boy. The gown is 34-inches long and 66-inches wide around the hem. It is made from white cotton and decorated with lace insertion. The entire bodice of the gown is lace insertion worked in a floral eyelet pattern. The sleeves are puffed ever so slightly, and the cuffs are made of the same insertion as the bodice. The bodice closes in the back with three buttons and a tie. The collar is trimmed with 1-inch wide insertion in a different pattern. The tucked skirt bottom is clipped, folded and stitched into a triangular shark's tooth pattern. The alternating triangles of shark's teeth and tucks are each 6^1/$_2$-inches long and 3^3/$_8$-inches deep. The individual "teeth" are 1-inch at the base and ^{1}/$_2$-inch high. The gown was probably made in the mid 1890s.

{ *Transferred from the Allen Memorial Art Museum, Oberlin College, Oberlin, Ohio. Gift of Mrs. C.A. Barden and Mrs. Harold Henderson, 1949, 1995.17.323* }

Point d'esprit and Lace TRIANGLES DRESS

"Fine laces—those which are generally known as net top laces—will be much used for the construction of yokes, chemisettes and guimpes. For these the all-over lace is better, while flouncing to match is used for sleeves. Narrow ruffles of fine lace, and all-overs and dotted net are used for the elbow sleeves of handsome costumes, a cap of the dress material or a short, slashed sleeve falling partly over the lace sleeve."

—The Ladies' Home Journal, "The New Spring Trimmings," (April 1907)

Layers of lace triangles applied beneath the round yoke give a sense that this dress is in constant motion—an Edwardian lady perhaps flitting about her social circles. Pouring V-shaped trim from a circular yoke was a relatively common practice in dressmaking at the time; this piece takes the design concept to extremes with lovely results. The piece dates from around 1905. The main fabric, as well as the base fabric for the triangles is a *point d'esprit* or a dotted netting. The bodice has a high-standing collar band edged at the top in gathered, lace edging that has a geometric zigzag pattern of enlarged *point d'esprit* dots. A lovely coordinate to the main fabrication, the edging is paired with a matching insertion, which trims the 2-inch wide neckband at the top just below the edging and at the base. These strips of insertion are simply straight stitched on top of the band. A short cut of the insertion is folded over the edge of the opening at the back of the neckband to serve as a placket. On the opposite side, the gathered lace edging continues from the top edge around the back opening of the band. The seam is covered with a strip of the insertion, straight stitched and with raw edges turned under; the neckline closes with three metal snaps. A faced placket continues into the body of the gown, which closes with hooks and eyes. The round gown yoke has the same coordinate laces appliquéd in seven triangular points radiating from the base of the collar. The yoke is outlined in the lace edging trimmed on both sides with the gathered edging. The full pouter-pigeon bodice is covered with three layers of delicate triangles cut from the same *point d'esprit* as the dress with each triangle edged in the same $1/2$-inch laces as decorate the collar. The headers of the laces are slightly overlapped and straight stitched. The first row of triangles is stitched at the bottom of the yoke and the remaining two layers are sewn to the bodice proper. Each layer has 16 triangles that are 6-inches

long with a 3-inch base. The sleeves are made from four alternating layers of lace-trimmed *point d'esprit* with the first and third layers made up of the triangles and the second and fourth layers simple ruffles. These are stitched to a short white cotton under sleeve. The skirt has two areas of shirring with the first one beginning at the waistband with seven rows of slight shirring $1/2$-inch apart. The second area of shirring begins 5-inches below the other and has six rows of shirring $1/2$-inch apart. The skirt has a slight train, and the bottom 12-inches has a similar lace appliqué pattern as the yoke. This time it is larger in scale and in a specific, uninterrupted zigzag design mitered at each point. Here the triangles are $7^{1}/_{2}$-inches at the base and $8^{1}/_{2}$-inches long. One and a half inches from the bottom of the gown is a strip of insertion edged on both sides with gathered edging; it incorporates the turned back hem. There is a white cotton under dress with an attached ruffle at the hem decorated with alternating rows of lace insertion and bias cut cotton. The lace is $1/2$-inch wide, and the bias cotton strips are $1^{3}/_{4}$-inches wide. At the top ruffle insertion, which would presumably receive the most stress, a $3/_{8}$-inch lip of fabric was left untrimmed and simply hand whipped to keep it from raveling.

{ Silverman/Rodgers Collection, 1983.1.241 }

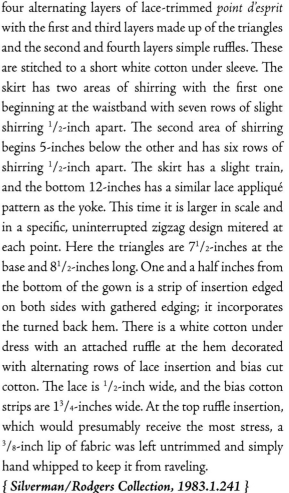
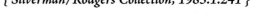

Blue & White Stripes
AND CHAMBRAY ENSEMBLE

"A skirt of the wash variety should be well-fitted at the waist-line, and the lower edge of the waist-belt should fit up snugly around the curve of the waist-line and not sag down. The waistband itself is better when made of the regular belting ribbon, and it should have two sets of hooks sewed upon it, two hooks for the first fastening, and then—about half an inch away—one more hook."

—The Ladies' Home Journal, "Mrs. Ralston's Chat," (June 1905)

Crisp and fresh, this two-piece dress was probably made by loving hands at home around 1900. Several details suggest the wearer preferred a less eclectic, somewhat practical approach to dressing—the striped fabric with its crisp hand, the banded finish and rigid pintucks tailoring the eyelet trim, and the contrast topstitching throughout. The combination fabrics are cotton, woven in blue and white stripes, trimmed with blue chambray. The high neckline and the cuffs are strips of eyelet insertion bordered by $^1/_2$-inch bands of chambray. The bands are cut on the straight of grain. The sleeves are long and slightly full with a placket in the underarm seam that closes with

two snaps on the cuff. Both sleeves have a gusset under the arm. Residual scalloped stitch marks near the cuffs indicate that at one time both had Maderia appliquéd decoration in the same pattern as on the skirt's hem. Perhaps the original shaped trim at the cuff pushed the level of embellishment beyond the point of comfort for the more conservative wearer. The front of the bodice has a heart-shaped, set-in panel of blue chambray that is topstitched and decorated with pearl buttons to create a mock shirt effect. Above the blue panel is an area of white cotton batiste decorated with five vertical pintucks and bordered on each side with eyelet insertion. There are two deep pleats on either side of the center front and center back that begin at the shoulder and continue to the waistband. There is also a pleated 3-inch peplum stitched into the waistband at the bottom. The bodice opens down the back and closes with hooks and eyes and three hidden buttons. The skirt is constructed of five panels with a waistband and is bordered with blue chambray in a scalloped pattern. This Madeira appliquéd border is secured with three rows of machine topstitching in contrasting thread. The entire dress is machine stitched except for the very bottom hemline border where the chambray is turned under and hand stitched. The shoulder seams are French; the remaining seams are raw.

{ *Gift of Martha McCaskey Selhorst, 1996.58.211ab* }

Cream Piqué Coat
WITH LEAF MOTIF INSERTION

"The fine ribbed piqué is always in vogue for children's short clothes. The little piqué coats are particularly pretty . . . For the very dressy little persons who can afford two coats, the best one for midsummer is pretty made of all-over Swiss or muslin embroidery worn over a separate slip of India silk."

—The Ladies' Home Journal, "Mrs Ralston's Chat About Children's Clothes," (July 1906)

Throughout earlier centuries, fine ribbed piqué was a common fabrication for children's coats. This example in creamy white piqué is from the fourth quarter of the 19th century and is trimmed with a wide embroidered insertion sporting a well-defined leaf motif giving the sense that little ones are happiest outdoors. The coat is 17^1/$_2$-inches long from the collar to the hem and the sleeves are 11-inches from the shoulder seam to the cuff. The embroidered insertion at the cuffs and the hem is white work. Actually, three types of trims are used. The hem and cuffs are finished in scalloped edging that is decorated with small flowers. The adjacent insertion is 1^1/$_2$-inches wide and worked in larger leaves and flowers. This insertion is also used vertically at the center of each pocket and is mitered at the bottom point. The third whitework edging is ^{3}/$_8$-inch wide and is used around the pockets and on the front of the sleeve cuff. Curiously, although the scalloped edging goes around the cuff, the other trimmings are used only on the fronts of each sleeve. The jacket closes with five large white buttons. Straight of grain muslin binding is used to cover the neckline and all of the joins of the insertion.
{ *Transferred from the Allen Memorial Art Museum, Oberlin College, Oberlin, Ohio. Gift of Helen Hildner, 1951, 1995.17.753* }

Green Silk
GAY NINETIES DRESS

"Pretty little jackets are numerous, and show great diversity of style and shape. Some are made quite plain, and have a shaped braided pattern all round and up each front; others are made in coat fashion with smart little turned-down collars, breast pockets and the back arranged like a gentlemen's morning coat. Others again have pleated backs, and the fronts crossed with gimp ornaments and hanging cords, and these have immensely high plain collars. Walking-costumes are still generally made with long-waisted bodices coming down into a point in front and cut shorter over the hips; there are often four small points in front."

—*Saturday Evening Post,* "Latest Fashion Phases," (June 1985)

Despite the touch of lace at the neckline and decorated hem, this afternoon costume worn prior to the turn of the 20th century leaves a decidedly masculine impression. The cut-away lines of the bodice combined with the somber olive hue of the silk reflects the residual influence of Charles Poynter, who is credited in *A History of Fashion* (1980 Orbis Publishing) as creating a sensation in Paris in the mid 1880s with his tailor-mades. These consisted of slightly feminized male jackets and rather plain skirts with fullness in back. This particular afternoon costume is made from rich silk moiré and golden yellow silk faille. The bodice has full leg-o'mutton sleeves that are gathered at the shoulders. The sleeves have turned-back cuffs trimmed with yellow faille. The neckline has a high-standing collar that is made from olive green velvet with the closure decorated with two pieces of gathered fabric that simulate a winged bow. Wide reveres drape (or lapel) folds down the bodice fronts exposing the faille lining. The center front of the velvet collar is gathered and comes to a slight point. The bodice opens at the side front covering the hooks and eyes at the center front of the under bodice. There is a yellow silk panel sewn directly under the neck that

is covered with lace and attached on the left side of the garment. A fabric belt applied to the inside of the garment is a revelation to the garment's origins. The London designer's signature, "Fredéric," followed by the address, "15 Lower Grosvenor Place, Eton Square S.W.," is woven into the belt in gold thread. Adjacent to the gold print, the date 1895 is roughly embroidered in red straight stitch, and indeed, the skirt has the full shape and train one would attribute to costume of the 1890s. The skirt with its train is made from eight panels of the green silk and is lined with a layer of white cotton. Two small gores add width to the center back at the hem. A pleated and draped hem flounce of the green and yellow silks is backed by a pleated taffeta silk flounce in a softer shade of yellow.

{ *Silverman/Rodgers Collection, 1983.1.189* }

Smocked Toddler's Dress
WITH ELONGATED EYELET TABS

"Smocking is daily gaining ground for indoor gowns of girls between the ages of four and fourteen, all the originality being displayed in the method of smocking, the shape the secured portions assume."

—Godey's Lady's Book, "The Fashions," (April 1888)

The classic look of geometric smocking on a high-yoke dress from the 1930s is made infinitely more interesting by three vertical strips of eyelet that are placed at the center and sides of the smocked panel. This dress is white cotton; the eyelet is machine embroidered with each strip finished in a point. The smocking is a combination of cable rows and trellises that create diamonds and zigzag effects. The back of the dress is decorated with insertion as well, but instead of smocking, the fullness is taken up with three $1/2$-inch tucks on either side of the center back where there is a placket with three buttons. Chain stitch embroidery decorates the collar and cuffs. The cuffs close with a button and loop.

{ *Gift of Martha McCaskey Selhorst Collection, 2003.35.9* }

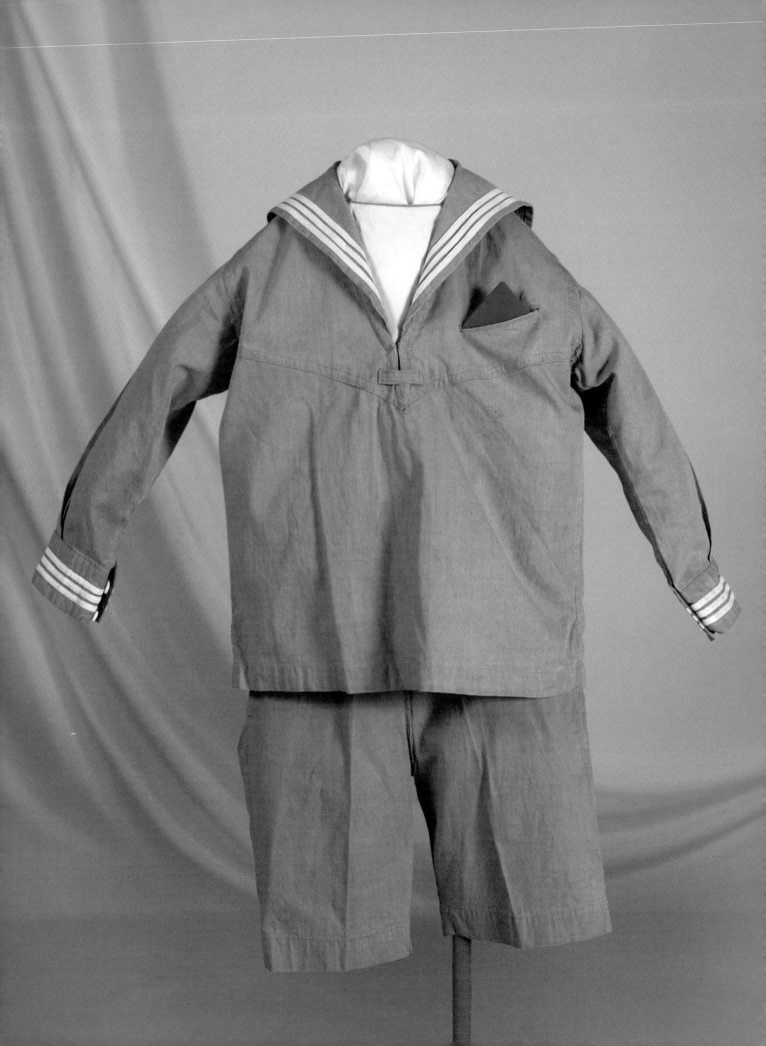

Little Boy's GOLD SAILOR SUIT

Nothing captures the sense of an Edwardian childhood quite like the little sailor suits made for boys and girls. They speak of summer fun in a garment made for ease of movement, unlike the usual children's clothing of the time. This charming little suit, from the late 19th or early 20th century, has a label that reads "Kaynee, Washtog, size 7" in the collar. The shirt is a typical shape and style that mimics a sailor's uniform. The red eagle and anchor appliqué on the left arm contains white chevrons. The left chest sports a welt pocket with a red handkerchief point. The sleeve and collar are trimmed with white piping. There are buttons on the sleeves and one button and button loop inside the collar. The pants have buttonholes that would have buttoned to an undershirt. The fall front facing was cut along the selvedge and there are little pockets on both sides. There is also a fly opening 2-inches long that is backed with a semicircle of matching fabric.

{ Gift of Martha McCaskey Selhorst Collection, 2003.35.3ab }

"*In slumbers of midnight the sailor-boy lay His hammock swung loose at the sport of the wind; But watch-worn and weary, his cares flew away And visions of happiness danc'd o'er his mind.*"

—*The Miscellany*, excerpt "The Mariner's Dream," (November 1805)

Blue & White
HONEYCOMB DRESS

"Take a measure around the throat, and around the chest and the shoulders, and cut the neck and the slope of the shoulders to correspond with these. Bend the elbow to measure the length of the arm, and cut the sleeve like that of a man's coat or make it straight and gather it into a wristband: make the arm-size loose, and let the sleeve enter it straightly—but not tight. The frock should reach to the knee—the edge hemmed to the depth of two inches."

—*The New England Farmer*, "Domestic Economy," (Aug. 1868)

Examples of printed fabrics date back as far as the Egyptian tombs, but the role prints played in mainstream fashion was significantly limited until the 19th century when manufacturing procedures made mass production viable. Even then, and into the early 20th century, prints were primarily accessible to the upper classes for daytime socializing. Because solid fabrics were easier to come by in earlier centuries, finding a print of any sort is indeed a treat. This particular polka dot is so uniformly printed it resembles a honeycomb pattern. The dark blue rim around the light blue dots, lending the fabric surface a sense of depth, further reinforces this effect. Like honey, the design elements are, indeed, sugar sweet. The neckline, cuffs and hip flounce are all decorated with an eyelet-embroidered insertion, as are the tucked panels that run down both center front and center back. The dress opens all the way down the center back and is closed with eight covered buttons on the bodice and three buttons on the skirt. The buttons are hidden behind the panel that matches the front of the dressmaking the back practically indistinguishable from the front. The dress dates from the 1920s and is approximately 27-inches long.
{ *Transferred from the Allen Memorial Art Museum, Oberlin College, Oberlin, Ohio. Gift of Mrs. F. C. Dudley, 1950, 1995.17.754* }

Day Dress
OF PRINTED BLACK & WHITE SILK

"Trimming is to play an important part in the new fashions. The effect will be gained not from how much trimming can be used upon a single costume, but from how harmonious the coloring is, how artistic the design of that which is selected; and of equal importance will be the way in which the trimming is posed upon the garment."

—*The Ladies' Home Journal*, "The New Spring Trimmings," (April 1907)

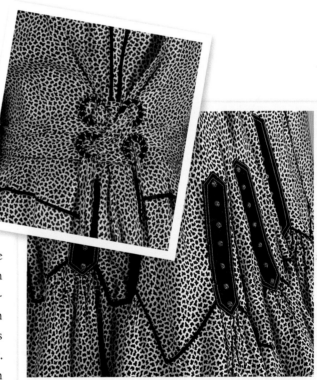

This black and white silk day dress has a remarkably modern print and is a striking example of a bold design used in a dress from about 1902. The bodice opens in the front and has a standing collar and center-front panel made of chemical lace. Black silk binding and tabs trimmed with tiny brass buttons add to the decoration on both the bodice and skirt. There's something very strong and almost mannish about the application of the tabs and the manner in which the waistline is drawn in by heavy lacing rather than gathers or pleats. The suffrage movement would have been building steam in the early part of the century, and such tailored detailing just might have reflected the wearer's strength of character. The top of the bodice, the upper sleeves and the skirt, all have points bound with black silk. Bishop sleeves end with tight cuffs decorated with black bands and buttons. The pouter pigeon front is pleated for added fullness and ends in a point at the center front waistband. The waistband fastening and four decorative pendants at the center back waist are decorated with rings covered in black and white silk cord. The skirt has a slight train. Ten small pintucks control the fullness of the bottom flounce of the skirt and are placed just below the tab-like black bands. *{Gift of Martha McCaskey Selhorst, 1996.58.341ab}*

Little Girl's MAROON SILK DRESS

"It is quite the fashion now for children's clothing to be made after nearly the same style as their elders; sometimes with an almost grotesque effect. Many little dresses are made with square Cardinal capes, of the same material as the dress, scarcely falling below the shoulders."

—*Arthur's Home Magazine,* "Toilet and Work-Table," (February 1869)

Vintage pieces, particularly children's garments, are rarely documented as to who wore them. This little dress is a treasure, indeed. We know that it is a re-made garment, and that it was worn by Mary Ruble Brown between 1886 and 1888. The family shared this much of its history upon its donation to the museum. In the "Ladies' Department" of the *New England Farmer,* a Monthly Journal, (Aug. 1868), Anne G. Hale writes of domestic economy. She notes that "Many persons when wishing for a change, or when their garments get a little defaced cut them over for their children; and so when purchasing things for themselves, keep their boys and girls in mind." Perhaps that was the case with this little dress.

It is burgundy silk lined with brown wool twill and decorated with machine-made lace along the pleated flounce that makes up the skirt. A self-fabric and lace bow is stitched in place at the center back and reflects the bustle style of an adult garment. The lining and the silk are sewn as one and there is both hand and machine stitching. The silk is pieced under both arms.

{ *Gift of Ada Brown and Eva B. Whetzel, 1987.6.1* }

Child's Swirls
OF BOBBIN LACE PETTICOAT

"As all skirts are made without an attached lining, a petticoat or drop skirt is a necessity. It is generally made to harmonize in color with the outer skirt. This is suitable for development in flannel of any kind and is mounted on a circular yoke of cambric. The lower part may be tucked and feather-stitched and edged with lace."

—*Pictorial Review*, "Underwear for Ladies and Children," (June 1905)

A child's wardrobe of undergarments would have undoubtedly included a number of petticoats—simple, everyday pieces layered beneath their skirts and dresses. This frilly example from around 1900 is white cotton with lace and white-work decoration. It is 17-inches long and 62-inches at the hem. It is entirely hand made, including the French seams. Above the fancy band is a section of 14 panels that are 3-inches wide separated by 1-inch lace insertion. The lace insertion design is somewhat of an abstract swirled motif. Each panel is hand embroidered with a stem holding four flowers. The bottom of the paneled section is finished with a strip of the same lace that separates them. The panels have a rolled and whipped edge attaching them to the lace. The hem, or fancy band, is decorated with a wider lace with a similar scrolling pattern that is more richly embellished with floral detail. It has a scalloped edge, and is gathered to create a flounce.

{ *Gift of Martha McCaskey Selhorst Collection, 2003.35.28* }

Little Girl's POLKA DOT & EYELET DRESS

"Little girls' gowns (that is, for those from three to six) are made in very simple style."

—The Cosmopolitan, "Fashions for Little Ones," (February 1887)

Several clues suggest that this was a summertime frock for a toddler. The eyelet is worked in a very airy pattern, the wide neckline is finished with a playful eyelet ruffle, and the sweet, capped sleeves leave much of the arm uncovered. Upon closer examination, it appears the design was either developed around the fabric—a polka dot jacquard—evidenced by the embroidered polka dots worked between the eyelet flowers. Or, perhaps the eyelet was worked and the fortunate seamstress happened upon a fabric to match—polka dots being a prevalent spring and summer motif.

The white-on-white polka dots are woven into the white jacquard fabric. The little dress is trimmed and decorated with hand-worked eyelet lace in a very open flower pattern. The bodice is made from alternating bands of the eyelet lace and the cotton. Narrower scalloped eyelet in the same pattern is used for the collar and the sleeves. The two cotton strips that alternate with the lace in the center front of the dress are tightly gathered in two places—midway down the bodice and right above the skirt—creating a puffed look popular in the 1880s. These shirred areas are backed with rectangular stays on the inside. Piping is used as a seam finish throughout—around the neckline, between the vertical strips on the bodice and to join the skirt to the body of the garment. The skirt is gathered at the waist and the eyelet lace at the bottom finishes $3^1/_2$-inches long and is scalloped at the edge. The join of the eye-

let to the skirt edge was finished by folding down to the right side the raw edge of the unadorned allowance at the top of the eyelet. The jacquard skirt edge was turned under. The eyelet was then layered under the skirt edge, intruding 1-inch into the skirt, and whipped in place on the inside and outside folds. The 1-inch shadowed effect created by the join appears to be a growth tuck. The dress opens at the back and has five buttons down the bodice. They are sewn on the left side and attached through the right. The waist seam is finished inside with a bias binding.

{ Silverman/Rodgers Collection, 1983.1.216 }

Brussels Bobbin & Needle
LACE SHAWL

"The laces this year are neither ecru or yellow, but just tea-tinted a soft and becoming tone. Point de Genes is one of the most useful kind of laces for ladies' and children's dresses in white and tea color, with a bobbin edge worked on a net foundation."

—Godey's Lady's Book, "The Fashions. A Monthly Resume of Practical Matters Relating to Dress and Social Events," (June 1888)

Shawls were among the most popular accessories in the mid-19th century. This one is from that time period and is a triangular shape worked in Brussels bobbin and needle lace appliquéd on machine-made net. The elegant and elaborate design is of feather plumes, flower arrangement ferns and greenery. { *Silverman/Rodgers Collection, 1983.1.1674* }

Tabbed SHOULDER CAPELET

"Picturesque styles predominate for children's clothes, and the great difficulty is to know when to stop being picturesque and become practical. After all, as children grow older the picturesque fashions are often the source of much unhappiness to them."

—*Harper's Bazaar*, "For the Children," (October 1901)

This sweet capelet exuding practicality and style, dates to about 1900. A child may have wished for cooler spring breezes as an excuse to drape this masterpiece over her shoulders. Few dresses would strike as charming an impression. It is made of creamy white piqué trimmed with three different eyelet edgings and light blue-green grosgrain ribbon. One eyelet pattern, 1¹/₂-inches wide, with a leaf and flower motif, runs down the center fronts and around the hem. Another forms trapezoidal tabs that hold the ribbon in place, and a third surrounds the neck. The capelet is in two sections, one for each arm, and is shaped at the shoulder with darts. The ribbon holds the two pieces of the capelet together.

{ *Transferred from the Allen Memorial Art Museum, Oberlin College, Oberlin, Ohio. Gift of the estate of Margaret Morfoot through Mrs. Robert Wheeler, 1973, 1995.17.1639* }

Baby's
BUTTERFLY AND JACQUARD BIBS

Made of white cotton embroidered with butterflies and flowers, and edged with Irish crochet, this delicate and well-used bib also has a triangular insertion of Irish crochet. The bib is tiny, only 5¼-inches long at the center front and 6-inches wide.

{ *Transferred from the Allen Memorial Art Museum, Oberlin College, Oberlin, Ohio. Gift of Beatrice Lanyi, 1970, 1995.17.343* }

This baby's bib from the early 20th century is made from a jacquard woven textile, woven to the shape of the bib. The charming image is of a stork delivering a precious basket to a little girl with a doll—a baby brother or sister brought down from the sky. The bib is 10³/₄-inches at the center front and 10¹/₂-inches wide.

{ *Transferred from the Allen Memorial Art Museum, Oberlin College, Oberlin, Ohio. Gift of Beatrice Lanyi, 1970, 1995.17.335* }

Turn of the Century
DIAPERS

Bloomingdale's Illustrated Catalog from 1886 contains an illustration of "Goodyear diapers" item numbers 610 and 611 sizes 2, 3 and 4 for 25 cents each, and sizes 5 and 6 for 29 cents. They are shaped much like these from the late 19th and early 20th centuries, except that each of the museum's examples has a buttonhole at the center back to fasten to an undershirt. Our number 316 is plain muslin decorated only with a ruffle at each leg. The 19-inch waist would indicate a child less than a year old. Our number 317 has a 20-inch waist and the muslin is gathered into the waistband to make it more accommodating. This diaper is trimmed with whitework edging at each leg. Each is essentially a triangle that has been shaped at the waist and at the sides to fit the waist and legs. The sides are then folded toward the center and buttoned to the apex, which is folded up to meet them. Because these are a single thickness of muslin, it would seem that they would be more effective as diaper covers than as what we think of today as diapers.

{ Transferred from the Allen Memorial Art Museum, Oberlin College, Oberlin, Ohio. Gift of Alice Little, 1948, 1995.17.316 }

{ Transferred from the Allen Memorial Art Museum, Oberlin College, Oberlin, Ohio. Gift of Mrs. G. W. Bailey through the Costume Institute of the Metropolitan Museum of Art, 1949, 1995.17.317 }

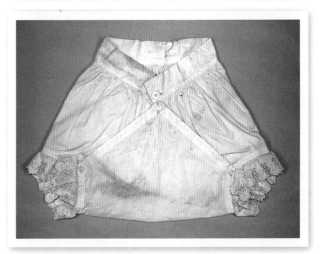

EMBROIDERIES

The embroidery designs shown are a sampling of the many patterns featured on the antique garments. These may be enlarged for hand embroidery or are available for machine embroidery (all formats) on CD-ROM from Martha Pullen Company.

Baby's Jacquard Bib

Silver Sequined
Ball Gown

Medallion and Daisies
Wedding Gown

Baby's Jacquard
Bib

Floral Vine
Christening Gown

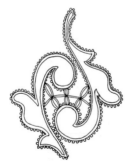

Medallion and Daisies
Wedding Gown

Bows and Lace
Afternoon Dress

Neo-Classic Greek Key
Ayrshire Christening Gown

Irish Crochet
Toddler Dress

Embroidered Bird
Baby Dress

Neo-Classic Greek Key
Ayrshire Christening Gown

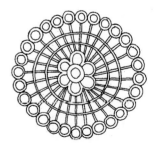

Tiers of Pink
Ruffles Dress

Embroidered Net
Dress

Bleeding Heart
Christening Gown

Irish Crochet
Toddler Dress

Bleeding Heart
Christening Gown

Neo-Classic Greek Key
Ayrshire Christening Gown

Floral Vine
Christening Gown

Baby's Butterfly
Bib

Ivory Net
Tea Dress

Wild Rose White
Piqué Coat

Baby's Butterfly
Bib

Baby's Jacquard
Bib

Filet Lace
Heirloom Peignoir

Embroidered Net
Dress

Baby's Jacquard
Bib

Neo-Classic Greek Key
Ayrshire Christening Gown

Embroidered Net
Dress

Filet Lace
Heirloom Peignoir

Silver Sequined
Ball Gown

Baby's Jacquard
Bib

Filet Lace
Heirloom Peignoir

Embroidered Bird
Baby Dress

Wild Rose White
Piqué Coat

Neo-Classic Greek Key
Ayrshire Christening Gown

Tiers of Pink
Ruffles Dress

Filet Lace
Heirloom Peignoir

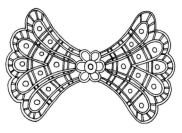

Tiers of Pink
Ruffles Dress

Filet Lace
Heirloom Peignoir

Irish Crochet
Toddler Dress

Wild Rose White
Piqué Coat

Filet Lace
Heirloom Peignoir

Bleeding Heart
Christening Gown

Medallion and Daisies
Wedding Gown